Sue,

Your loving kindness over the years means the world to me.

Blessings,
Sally Nitz

Sally Nitz

A Work in Progress

Triumphing Over Mental Illness

Tate Publishing & *Enterprises*

A Work in Progress
Copyright © 2010 by Sally Nitz. All rights reserved.

No part of this publication may be reproduced, stored in a retrieval system or transmitted in any way by any means, electronic, mechanical, photocopy, recording or otherwise without the prior permission of the author except as provided by USA copyright law.

All Scripture used is from the New International Version (NIV) of the Bible.

Some names have been changed per request. All members of the department of psychiatry have been referred to only by first names to protect their privacy.

This book is designed to provide accurate and authoritative information with regard to the subject matter covered. This information is given with the understanding that neither the author nor Tate Publishing, LLC is engaged in rendering legal, professional advice. Since the details of your situation are fact dependent, you should additionally seek the services of a competent professional.

Published by Tate Publishing & Enterprises, LLC
127 E. Trade Center Terrace | Mustang, Oklahoma 73064 USA
1.888.361.9473 | www.tatepublishing.com

Tate Publishing is committed to excellence in the publishing industry. The company reflects the philosophy established by the founders, based on Psalm 68:11,
"The Lord gave the word and great was the company of those who published it."

Book design copyright © 2010 by Tate Publishing, LLC. All rights reserved.
Cover design by Blake Brasor
Interior design by Joey Garrett

Published in the United States of America

ISBN: 978-1-61566-942-4
1. Self-Help / Mood Disorders
2. Self-Help / Anxieties & Phobias
10.03.02

Dedication

I dedicate this book to God and my parents, Albert and Donna, and to all those who believed in me when I didn't believe in myself.

Acknowledgements

First, and foremost, I would like to give credit, thanks, and praise to the triune God: Father, Son, and Holy Spirit. Without the workings of all three, I know I would be institutionalized. They give me the support and the inspiration to go on.

Secondly, I would like to thank my family. They hurt with me in those dark days, and their love carried me through. A special thanks filled with love is for my parents, Albert and Donna Nitz, for their unfailing love and devotion to me. I am indebted to them for raising me in a Christian home, where I learned from an early age the values that are so dear to me today. My brother, Daryl Nitz, has also been a source of support and encouragement to me. My aunt, Mary Kay, and uncle, John Warlop, have, since I was born, loved me unconditionally and believed in me more than I did myself. Their faith in me continues to lift me up and encourages me. My aunt, Kay, and uncle, Richard, McDowell saw the good in me. They loved me for who I was and encouraged me to become a chaplain. My uncle, Dale Starkey, and his girlfriend, Mary Grubbs, shared their hearts with me and were always in my corner. My aunt, Elizabeth Skinner, understood my struggles and wept for and with me through them. My aunt, Donna Guckeyson, was there with me since my birth and is always there in a crisis. My cousins and their families, whom I consider friends, have loved me and believed in me through it all: Alan, Suzanne, and Cady McDowell, Ram, Susan, Rajan, Maya, and Jay Mudambi, Wes, Lisa, and Luke Waters, Frank, Tara, and Kyle Rosselli, Eric and Ross Carper, Jill, Erica, Shane and Seth Hippli, John, Tami, and Justin Warlop, Lauren and Jeremy Campbell, Heather Taylor, Don and Ruth, Donna Rae, Cathy, Bob and Bonnie, Dennis and Joy, and Donnie Pressman, George and Rosemary Richards, and Paul and Carol Jursik. Although my two dear grandmothers are no longer with me physically, I feel their presence spiritually. I want to thank my grandma, Mildred Starkey, who gave me such wisdom, humor, and the ability to tell a story. My grandma, Elsie Nitz, gave me a sense to just "keep a-goin'" and not be concerned with being poor. Both women impressed on me their faith in God and his daily miracles in life.

Thirdly, I would like to thank all of my friends who stood by me through thick and thin and encouraged me to tell my story. Since I was in fifth grade, Pam Link Dobberstein befriended me and helped me see the humor in life. Through the years our friendship has grown to a deeper level. She understood my dark times and prayed for a return to the light. Later, her husband Reverend Paul Dobberstein also kept me in prayer and wished me the best. Deborah Vogel has been my friend since our first year of college together. She has shared in my mountaintop experiences as well as been there through the many valleys. Her husband, Glenn, and their daughters, Sonja, Elsa, and Hannah, have supported me in all I do. Linda Clark has been my friend since I began teaching at David Hill School. She is the consummate listener, encourager, and fellow dog lover. She is the first person I talk to almost every day. Her family has embraced me as one of their own: Mary Glenn, Jim, Brendan and Rachel, and Devin and Kristen, Porter and Doris, Gary and Mary Ellen, Jaret and Jaret Jr. Clark, and Katie Suchs. Amos, Abbey, Luka, Lily, Maytag, Carver, Dixie, and the latest addition, Ernestine Clark showed me love and the joys of a multi-dog household as did Bessie and Molly Glenn. Lucy Maple, another one of my teacher friends, has always given me a reality check and shared in my love for cats and other four-legged creatures.

Tyla Brown Sherman, my boss at Wonder World Child Development Center, gave me a job when no one else would. She shared with me her faith in God, and she encouraged me to do my best. She believed I would get better, and she trusted in God to make it happen. Without her support, I would have never made it out of my deepest depressions. Her encouragement is contagious. Her parents, Reverend Gus and Elaine Brown, have been my spiritual advisors. They have given me unending guidance in matters of the Spirit. Pastor, your deep understanding of mental illness made it possible for you to reach me when I was almost beyond hope. I'm glad God gave you this skill.

Thanks to all of my co-workers, the parents, and the children at Wonder World Child Development Center. You have made my years there a pleasure. The children infused my life with joy and laughter at a time when I found it difficult to find joy in living. Thank you for being yourselves and bringing out the best in me. A special thanks to: Darlene Ruple, Michelle Barclay, Kelvin Wade, Selema Christian, Nadine Bates, Nichole Greene, Lourdes Callahan, Chris Daood, James and Donna Wells, Barbara Mays, Annette Kolbs, Robin Pickett, Tiffany Lee, Tia Barry, Lynnette Williams, Shalonda Blackmon, Portia Stembridge, Sally and Kayla Sykes, Caroline Walker, Roscoe Fry, Evelyn and James Jenkins, Beth Greene, Bettye Christian, Louise Millender, Martha Trujillo, Ruth Garcia, Karen Mitchell, Lillian Alexander, Lori Sneed, and Nichole Shephard.

Drs. Ralph and Alice Darr helped me through the seemingly insurmountable task of getting my master's degree during some of the darkest days of my life. Their love and support buoyed my confidence in myself and my writing abilities. Thank you.

Janet (*Juanita*) *Lijerón* and *Manena Vidlak* not only taught me Spanish, but they inspired me to rise to new levels as a student and as a human being. *Les doy gracias a Uds. con cariños desde el fondo de mi corazón.*

The staff at West Akron Veterinary Clinic has not only done an outstanding job of caring for my pets with dignity and respect, but they have treated me the same way. They have ministered to my spirit in ways that have touched me deeply. I thank Dr. Anne Phlipot, Dr. Julia Brown-Herold, Dr. Frederick Keller, Sue Ringler, Jessi Llewellyn, and Tiffany Cook. Sue gives me invaluable advice, both personally and professionally, almost on a daily basis. I appreciate that more than these words can convey. Jessi's mom Mary Llewellyn, a real estate agent for Mosholder Realty, helped me see my dream of becoming a homeowner come to fruition. I appreciate her diligence in finding me the perfect home so quickly.

My former neighbors and old friends showed me kindness and compassion. Ray and Ramona Cicogna and Dave and Nila St. John kept me in prayer through all of my trials. John Graf forgave me and kept me from being arrested. The Hershberger family welcomed me to the neighborhood and greeted me on my daily walks with my dogs. Thank you: Joe, Betty, Mike, Dave, Catherine, Tyler, Marina, and Vita Dee. Dave, Kelly, Evan, and Toby Seiberling were equally friendly, and they showed concern about me and my family. Steve, Stephanie, Marie, and Steve Jr. Klein were also great neighbors who cared about me and my pet family.

Fourthly, I want to thank with all my heart the staff at Akron General Medical Center. Without their medical expertise, support, and encouragement, I could not find the strength to face each day. My psychiatrist, Dr. Seymour Jeffries, has been a consistent strength in my life. I greatly value his medical knowledge and ability to understand people. His wisdom has helped me out of many tough situations. I appreciate his willingness to really listen to me and help me take control of my illness. His secretary has also helped me navigate the bumps in the road, which were many. Her patience and understanding calmed me in times of trouble. She always has my best interest at heart. My general practitioner, Dr. Joseph Panzner, has not only been an excellent personal physician, but he had the insight to recommend me to Dr. Jeffries at a crucial time in my life. I know I can count on him whenever I am sick in any way. His bedside manner is beyond compare. For his help, I am eternally grateful. He and the staff at Copley Medical Group has not only kept me healthy but ministered to my spirit through their caring ways. I thank Dr. Robert Burns, Dr. John Kromalic, RNs Janet, Nancy, Judy, Denise, and Joanne, and the secretarial staff. Dr. Moshe Torem pinch-hit for Dr. Jeffries at critical moments and has been supportive of me over the years. He helped me greatly with being aware of reality and staying in it. The affirmations he taught me to write about myself have stayed with me over all these years. Dr. Lori Pittinger also substituted for Dr. Jeffries. Her happiness in my recovery bolstered my confidence. The way she treats patients with respect and dignity makes a difference. It did to me. Dr. Susan Ray of Northeast Ohio Nephrology Associates has been a superb nephrologist and friend. She celebrates in my recovery and inspires me to rise higher. Dr. Joseph Zebari and Dr. Chris Hines showed me kindness at a devastating time in my life. I appreciate their compassion and medical expertise.

Barbara Tucker has been a good friend to me since my first admission. She is an outstanding nursing assistant who really cares about patients. I am grateful that she cared about and for me when I was at my lowest point and beyond. Her wisdom and no-nonsense approach have been invaluable to me.

The nursing staff was instrumental in my recovery. Claudia was one of the first I remember. I have always been touched by her kindness and compassion for people and animals. Bekke not only believed in me, but she trusted me to come to her house to do a clean-up job. That trust gave me every confidence that I was getting better. The other nurses that helped me were Jeff, Grace D., Grace G., Dave, Helen, Diane, Cathy, Jaimie, Mark, Paul, Pat S., Ed, Vince, Kathy, Rae, Karen, Marlene, Constance, Sue, and Leslie. The support staff that gave me encouragement was Becky, Heidi, Cheryl, Pete, Susan, Nancy P., Nancy N., Larry,

Rhonda, Kathy S., Kathy W., Duane, Deb, Kathy Sh., Jerry, and Russ. Joel, the security guard, was there to help at one of my most desperate moments. His patience and understanding were invaluable.

The staff that I've come to know since becoming a chaplain has also encouraged me, and they accepted me as a colleague. The nurses are Leanne, Brenda, Lindsay, Deb, Debbie, Pat G., Lisa, Pam, Lea, Sarah, Jazzlynn, Theresa, Sari, and Catherine. The support staff is Kim, Kathleen, Joanna, Tyrell, Felice, Fran, Lee, Patty, Darcell, Marie, Yolanda, April, Brian, Barb, Augusta, Patrick, Kyle, Adam, Ira, Tamara, Jessica, Tia, John, Belinda, Lana, Terri, Kelly, Bobbie Jo, and both Steves.

While all of the employees on the psychiatric units at Akron General have helped me immensely through their kindness and friendship, many have given me a bonus by being my friend outside the hospital. Kathleen has supported and promoted me in all of my ventures. She became my biggest sewing client and brought me much business. She attended one of my seminars and brought her daughter, Kali, and a friend. But most of all, she encouraged me to tell my story. Thanks Kathleen.

Susan reached out to me not only when I was a patient but later when I became a chaplain as well. She sees my potential and helps me realize it. To her, I was more than just another patient. That meant the world to me and still does. Thank you Susan.

Others who gave me friendship and support outside

of the hospital in starting my nonprofit organization and/or by coming to my housewarming were: Jaimie and Lindsay, Claudia, Barbara, Bekke, Brenda, Karen, Nancy, Kathy S., Kathleen, Susan, Becky, Heidi, Jim Franklin, Reverend Lin Barnett, Deb Dockery, Paul Hawkins, Charlotte Ragan, and Joey De Barr. I can't thank you enough for celebrating with me in my recovery and independence. All of you looked beyond my past and saw my future. Thank you from the depths of my being.

To all of the patients I've ministered to at Akron General, I am indebted to you for sharing your lives with me and allowing me to be a part of it. You have given back to me more than I could ever give to you. You prompted and encouraged me to take my story to a broader audience. I will never forget you.

I want to thank Alan Bleyer, former CEO, for managing and directing Akron General Medical Center. His leadership helped to make my recovery possible by putting all of the right people in place at the right time.

My CPE friends, also from Akron General, were instrumental in my full recovery. First, I'd like to thank Reverend Lin Barnett for giving me a chance to prove myself as a chaplain. His encouragement along the way gave me strength. He and his wife, Reverend Kim, supported me through it all. Joey DeBarr and Kate Valentine gave me wise counsel and guidance. Eileen Schonfeld shared her wisdom with kindness. She and her husband, Steve, also gave me employment caring for their beloved dog, Max. Charlotte Ragan was the chaplains' chaplain. She always made time to listen to my problems.

In my first unit (2004–2005), I thank from the core of my being: Barbara Rose, Deb Dockery, Marilyn Mihalic, Mary Hunter, Luann Youngman, Lorie Lerner, and Reverend Charlie Cooper. In my second unit (2005–2006), I thank Father Patrick Allala, Reverend H. Paul Schwitzgebel, and Reverend Chuck Mills. In my third unit (2006–2007), I thank Rachel Stinson, Paul Hawkins, Betty Budyka, and Joann Harris. In my fourth, and final, unit (2007–2008), I thank Eileen Cousino and Reverend Joseph Horton.

To all of my other chaplain friends, I thank Judy Baughman, Marianne Worley, Kathy Schen, Reverend Nan Taylor, Mark Ballard, Mike Prendergast, Father Vasyl Marchak, Reverend Wally Anderson, Reverend Lynne Thompson-Bryant, Tim Short, Elizabeth Armstrong, and Jim Scalf. I also thank all of the other Akron General employees who have shown me kindness over the years. You have shown me that a little kindness goes a long way.

Many people outside of Akron General helped me in beginning Celebrate Life Ministries, Inc. in February 2007. I am forever grateful for your belief and trust in me. Thank you: Reverend Gus and Elaine Brown, Helen Butler, Jim and Linda Clark, Brendan and Rachel Clark, Devin and Kristen Clark, Dee Curci, Fred and Diana Doerr, Mary Glenn, Paul and Carol Jursik, Kathryn Krautwurst, Elaine Lewis, Lucy

Maple, Albert and Donna Nitz, George and Rosemary Richards, Rose Rose, Deborah Snyder, Curt, Tina, and Julia Thomas, Larry Thompson, Deborah and Sonja Vogel, John and Mary Kay Warlop, John and Tami Warlop, James and Donna Wells, and Roger and Barbara Wells.

The people who came to or helped with my seminars shared their lives with me in a deep way that encouraged me to plan for the next one. My heartfelt thanks to: Reverend Gus Brown, Barbara Tucker, Albert Nitz, Sandra Modrick, Sheila Napolitano, Lillian Alexander, Lee and Paula Holmes, Chris Daood, Murphy Smith, Barbara Wells, Donna Wells, Betty Kuhns, Maria Kubalak, Ellen Mc Sweeney, Jan Hoover, and Kathryn Krautwurst.

The staff at David Hill School supported me before, during, and after my first breakdown. They were not only my colleagues but they were friends in times of trouble. I thank: Barbara Whaley, Murielene White, Linda Clark, Lucy Maple, Phil Vincente, Rita Hosch, Margaret Moran, Sheila Green, Elaine Lewis, Barb Allen, Anna Mae Parker, Geneva Shedrick, Larry Griffin, Mike Burt, Bill Atkinson, Pauline Gordon, Jim Phillips, Alice McNeil, Ann Griffith, Marge Chop, Mike Stallworth, Earl Van Pelt, and Carl Lambert and Chuck Linderman.

Bill Siegferth, president of Akron Education Association, was instrumental in helping me obtain my disability from State Teachers Retirement System. I am grateful to him for his efforts at a time when

I could barely function. STRS has taken care of me financially since 1995. If I didn't have their support, I'd be living well below the poverty level. Thank you STRS for all you have done and are doing for me. I appreciate it more than words can convey.

The congregation at Akron Alliance Fellowship gave me love and respect when I didn't have them for myself. They showed me that loving a sinner is the only way to truly show God's love. I especially thank: Jeremy and Alexis Sherman, Ernest Calhoun, Roger and Barbara Wells, James and Donna Wells, Jasper and Elyse Fambro, Victor, Liz, Mariah, Victoria, and Victor Jr. Eaves, Christine Motley, Charles and Annie Beecher, Michael, Tangi, Richard, and Micah Delaney, Ken and Gwen Walker, George and Yvonne Pringle, Deborah Snyder, Gregory Neal, Bill and Fannie Brown, Glenn, Beth, Nichole, Talia, Kia, and Kira Greene, Cierra Price, Taraya and Terell Rucker, Roscoe and Arella Fry, Dwight and Vickie Williams, Keziah Buchanan, Mary Wilkerson, Glenda Brown, Sharon Easterling, Crystal, Donte, and Dorian Hooks, Donovan Mines, Melvin and Lynn Gaines, Marnell and Nate Riles, Aaron and Taylor Lane, Lee and Paula Holmes, Larry Johnson, Georgia McLaughlin, and Carrie Sneed.

The people I've met through Haven of Rest Ministries, Inc. have shown me kindness, love, and compassion through it all. I thank: Reverend Curt and Eileen Thomas, Valerie and Cliff Schmidt, Curt, Tina, and Julia Thomas, Reverend Ben and Kathy

Walker, Kathy Wells, Rose Rose, Doris Krueger, Emma Reusch, Mary Jordan, Dorothy and Johnny Hullum, Jan Pluck, Gary Meeks, Karen Wren, Angela and Greg Stewart, Pat and Kay Blanc, Ben Pheneger, Larry and Pauline Coldiron, Geoff, Amy, and Brooke McElhattan, Jackie Trent, Barb Wilkie, Wynette Carmichael-Harper, Leah Gibson, Myra Schneider, Matt Pryor, Andy Kidd, Margaret and Fred Duncan, Velma Brimston, Chris Ehlert, Melvin and Twyla Fields, Renee Green, Pat Marr, Sandy Kibler, Pat Yorkie, Jim and Sandy Butler, Pat Tressel, Jack Hugg, Larelle Whetsell, Chris Morgan, Dave and Sherry Shew, and Sandy Gale.

My colleagues at Akron's Children's Hospital gave me encouragement and support during my brief tenure there. A special thanks to Reverend Karen Ballard, Sally Katz, Kevin Carr, Father Patrick Allala, and the nursing staff on 8100. Julie RN believed in me and my ideas for a nonprofit organization. Thanks, Julie, your enthusiasm put me on the right path.

I'd like to thank Tate Publishing for believing in me and putting my story in book form and distributing it nationwide. Their staff was invaluable in the process. Stacy Baker, Sara Wood, Rachael Sweeden, Dave Dolphin, Curtis Winkle, and Lauren Downen made my introduction to the publishing world nearly effortless. I want to give a special thanks to Kathleen Knapp for her tireless work in skillfully editing my manuscript and to Blake Brasor for his efforts in designing the cover. I thank the Layout and Design Department for their work in getting my manuscript ready to print and seeing the final product come to life. I thank the Marketing Department for their work in helping me sell my book and taking it to new audiences.

I thank Heidi Larew for all of her help in the process of writing this book and for allowing me to use a picture of her sculpture. I am indebted to Dr. Jennifer Durham for so graciously writing the foreword. I thank Judy Knight from Akron General Medical Center's Medical Library for her kind assistance in supplying resource materials.

Dr. James Cannatti and Amy RN of Summit Opthalmology have not only skillfully and graciously monitored my vision but have rejoiced with me in my vision to help others. Thank you to the staff of Summit Opthalmology.

Dr. Karen Kellogg of Fairlawn Foot and Ankle Clinic encouraged me in my work as a chaplain and believed I could do anything I set my mind to. Her faith in me inspired me to strive to do better. I thank her and her staff for literally and figuratively putting me on the right path.

I am grateful to Vicki Thomas of Quick Photo for taking the photo of my pet family in 2000 and to Dan Liddle, the owner, for scanning it along with other pictures for this book. I thank Andy Pfaff of Lyons Photography for beautifully taking the photo for the back cover and for skillfully taking my current photo of my pet family. Thanks to Chrissy's Paw Spa for making Destiny look like a purebred dog for that photo. I thank Pat Burke for her help in cutting and styling my hair.

Many thanks to those who wrote endorsements for this book: Heidi Larew, Reverend Lin Barnett, Jeff RN, and Dr. Ralph Darr. Thanks for believing in me.

Last, but certainly not least, I thank all of my wonderful pets, who have stood beside me through all of the ups and downs and loved me unconditionally. They inspire me to be the best possible human I can be. They are Cinnamon, Butterscotch, Tawny, Destiny, Spitfire, Rudy, Baby, Codie, Nugget, Sugar Pie, Suzy Q, and, the latest addition, Provi.

Table of Contents

Foreword	27
Introduction	29
Beginnings	37
A Life in Crisis	41
The Need for Hospitalization	45
Life after Teaching	55
Pet Therapy	61
Human Support System	71
Everyday Living	97
Combating Episodes	101
Criminal at Large	105
Day-to-Day Living	113
Home versus Hospitalization	117

Homeward Bound	121
Dealing with Mental Illness	125
Focus on the Future	129
Daily Grace	139
The Success Principle	145
The Upside of Living	157
Epilogue	163

Foreword

By Jennifer Durham

Throughout history, children have been raised on tales of heroes and heroines, men and women who answer the call to adventure armed with only wit and the will to triumph over adversity. In emotional infancy, they set off into the mythical wilderness. It is only through the felling of giants, the meeting of opponents human and divine, and the mastery over misfortunes that they emerge victorious, mature, worthy of the prize.

As I read Sally Nitz's *A Work in Progress,* I am reminded of the archetypal hero's journey. How often the most epic battles and darkest adventures unfold on the landscape of one's own mind. Sally's personal journey through mental illness inspires the reader to search for meaning in life's uncertainties and despair. It illuminates the treasures that can only be found in testing. It affords us the opportunity to discover allies and armorers who would otherwise pass from our lives unnoticed.

Sally's story is truly a heroine's tale, an expedition into the wilderness of the human psyche. Through Sally's trials and triumphs, the reader will come to discover hope, healing, and the hero within.

—Dr. Jennifer Durham, Director
New Beginnings Counseling Center
Wooster, Ohio
Durham-Larew Leadership Resources
Akron, Ohio

Introduction

For those who have a limited knowledge of mental illness, I have included a detailed description of the diseases that afflicted me: bipolar disorder and obsessive-compulsive disorder (OCD).

Bipolar Disorder

Bipolar disorder (manic-depressive illness) affects more than 10 million adults in the United States.[1] It is an emotional/mental disorder which is characterized by extreme highs and lows in mood. Periods of normalcy occur in between. The disease is the result of a chemical imbalance in the brain and often runs in families. The average age of onset is in the early twenties. Both men and women are affected.

According to the National Institute of Mental Health (NIMH), the symptoms of mania include increased energy, activity, and restlessness; excessively high, euphoric mood; extreme irritability; racing thoughts, talking very fast, and jumping from one idea to another; distractibility, inability to concentrate well; little need for sleep; unrealistic belief in one's abilities or powers; poor judgment; spending sprees; a lasting period of behavior that is different from usual; increased sex drive; abuse of drugs, alcohol, and sleeping medications; provocative, intrusive, or aggressive behavior; and/or denial that anything is wrong.[2]

The symptoms of depression include lasting sad, anxious, or empty mood; feelings of hopelessness or pessimism; feelings of guilt, worthlessness, or helplessness; loss of interest in activities once enjoyed, including sex; decreased energy, a feeling of fatigue or of being slowed down; difficulty concentrating, remembering, or making decisions; restlessness or irritability; sleeping too much or inability to sleep, change in appetite and/or unintended weight loss or gain; and/or thoughts of death or suicide, or suicide attempts.[3]

Not only are some of these symptoms present, but breaks in reality may also occur. This leads to impulsive behavior and poor judgment. The delusions, however, seem very real, even logical, to the person experiencing them. These incidents can greatly affect relationships with others and work production. Without a support system, the bipolar individual is left to follow his/her often misguided impulses. Episodes of depression cause a person to feel hopeless and without motivation, whereas episodes of mania cause a person to feel on top of the world and indestructible. A false sense of security ensues.

If on medication, a person may feel so good that s/he stops taking it. Dealing with adverse side effects such as weight gain and sluggishness may also cause a person to stop taking medication. Some individuals try self-medicating with alcohol, street drugs, or prescription medications. In addition, the stigma of the illness and the difficulty of diagnosis cause many people having the illness to go untreated.

Of those treated, staying on medication is essential to mental stability. Detecting the problem is only part of the equation. Maintaining the proper chemical balance is a matter of trial and error. The psychiatrist has to prescribe the medicine best thought to treat the illness. Side effects may cause the desired medicine to lose its effect. Lithium, for example, is a widely used bipolar medicine. It has kidney damage as one of its side effects. It is necessary to have a psychiatrist who is well-versed in pharmacology to ensure that medicines do no damage to other organs.

Once treated, the bipolar person can lead a productive life. It is essential, however, for him/her to be in touch with his/her body to circumvent problems when they arise. Seeking health care at the onset of problems can avoid a major episode.

An episode differs from what is popularly termed a "nervous breakdown." Nervous breakdowns result from a system overload brought on by stress. Usually, following a period of rest, a person can return to normal. A bipolar episode, on the other hand, requires medication and usually psychotherapy to be overcome. A regimen of medication on a consistent basis rectifies the chemical imbalance. This is not an easy task. All medication, including over-the-counter drugs, affects the emotional/mental makeup of the individual.

There are four types of bipolar disorder, according to the Diagnostic and Statistical Manual of Mental Disorders IV (DSMIV). The first is Bipolar I Disorder, which is characterized by manic or mixed episodes lasting at least seven days that require hospitalization. Usually the mania is followed by depression lasting at least two weeks. The second is Bipolar II Disorder, which is characterized by a pattern of depressive episodes and a shifting back and forth with hypomania but is not a full-blown manic episode. The third is Bipolar Disorder Not Otherwise Specified (BP-NOS), which is used when the person has symptoms that do not meet the criteria of Bipolar I or II. The symptoms may not last long enough or the person has too few symptoms; however, the symptoms are out of the ordinary for that person. The fourth is Cylothymic Disorder or Cyclothymia which is a mild form of bipolar disorder. These people have episodes of hypomania that shift back and forth with mild depression that lasts for two years or more.[4] The type of bipolar disorder referred to in this book is Bipolar I.

Obsessive-compulsive Disorder (OCD)

Obsessive-compulsive Disorder (OCD) is an anxiety disorder that is characterized by obsessions followed by compulsions that the person thinks will rid him/her of the obsession. The obsession is a recurring, unwanted thought. The compulsion is an act or ritual performed after the obsession in hopes of preventing the obsession or making it go away. The compulsion provides only temporary relief from the obsession. OCD affects 2.2 million adults in the United States. It can be treated with medication and exposure-based psychotherapy.[5]

The OCD sufferer thinks compulsively of an idea that is difficult to remove from his/her thought processes. It can be a fear of being contaminated by germs. It can be a thought that one is unsafe. It can also be a thought of having committed a bad act or crime that is what is portrayed in this book. The rituals or compulsions may be repeatedly washing one's hands to rid oneself of germs. It could be repeatedly locking a door or checking the stove to see that it is off. I did not really have any rituals that I performed to get rid of my obsessive thoughts. I just went over my obsession over and over again. The more I went over it, the bigger it became. Once I even took photographs to the police station convinced that there was something there to expose me for the criminal I thought I was. Of course, there was nothing suspicious in them.

Repeating a given act is the only thing that brings relief to the individual with OCD before medical treatment. For me, a prescription of an antipsychotic helped. Psychotherapy is also beneficial. Through this therapy, an individual can learn techniques to combat the illness. Stress and life's problems, however, can lead to the onset of an OCD episode. If the stress is great, it can overcome the effects of the medication. Every time my medication stopped working, I would have to be hospitalized. During that time, my psychiatrist would try different medications. It usually took over two weeks to find the proper balance.

Life Before Mental Illness

Before I had mental illness I was basically a happy person. I loved my work as an elementary school teacher and spent much of my free time doing school work. When I wasn't doing that I enjoyed sewing and reading mysteries. My favorite mystery writer was P.D. James, a British writer. Her novels were rich in new vocabulary and her plots spell-binding. She took mysteries to a new level for me. Previously, I had read Sir Arthur Conan Doyle's Sherlock Holmes and Agatha Christie's Miss Marple. I loved watching Joan Hickson play Miss Marple on the PBS series. I still often re-watch my favorites. But P.D. James has a unique way of telling a story which kept me captivated. I kept checking the bookstore to see when she came out with a new book.

I also enjoyed listening to R & B music. My favorite groups were The Spinners, The Four Tops, and Kool and the Gang. My favorite solo artists were Luther

Vandross, Whitney Houston, and Anita Baker. I had listened to The Spinners ever since I was in my mid-teens and saw "Roots" on television. I couldn't believe what Caucasian Americans had done to the African Americans. It was a rude awakening for me. Consequently, I began to vicariously immerse myself in African American culture. I did this through music, literature, and television. It was not until December 1980 that I moved from Elgin, Illinois where I grew up with few African American friends to Akron, Ohio which had a large African American population that I could immerse myself physically.

Most of my bosses were African Americans as were many of my co-workers. I began to make friendships that were enduring. I worked at an inner-city bank, elementary school, rescue mission, and later, a daycare. I began to go to an African American church about the time of my illness. I can honestly say that the African Americans I have come to know have shown me more love and compassion than many Caucasians I know outside of most of my family.

This story chronicles my descent into madness, my struggle to get better, and my eventual triumph over mental illness. The journey was, at times, dark, but the end product was well worth the trials. I hope the reader enjoys reading the story as much as I did writing it. I am constantly improving and getting to know my disease better. As I stand today, I remain: a work in progress.

—Sally Nitz
Akron, Ohio
November 2009

Beginnings

> It was good for me to be afflicted so that I might learn your decrees.
>
> Psalm 119:71

Andrae Crouch sings, "I didn't think it could be, 'til it happened to me," in regard to salvation in Jesus Christ.[1] I've felt that way with my whole bipolar experience. I was diagnosed with bipolar disorder in March 1991, when I was thirty years old. I was teaching second grade at the time and in a stressful marriage. I was a workaholic—staying late at school, taking papers to grade when my husband and I went out to dinner, and staying up until all hours working on school stuff.

Before my first actual breakdown, I had noticed some signs that I was in trouble. Although I loved my job, I would cry at times on my way to work. I would even get emotional seeing a school bus picking up children for school. School, you see, was everything to me.

In addition, I had an argument with a colleague that became verbally abusive. It bothered me because angry outbursts were not in my nature, and for the first time, I considered seeing a psychiatrist. But when I told my mom about my feelings, she said I just needed to "get right with the Lord."

In a way she was right. Spiritually, I was at a low point. I had entered into a marriage that was one-sided. I went through with the marriage out of a sense of guilt over the pre-marriage violations my spouse and I had been involved in. Although I was a "technical virgin" at the time of the wedding, we had allowed oral sex to be the high point of our relationship. There was no undoing of the shame that followed me for years to come. Many people don't call sexual sin "sin." I knew what I was doing was wrong, but I continued to do it. I made excuses to myself. I had so much wanted to have a boyfriend that I compromised my principles. Living in sin greatly affected my psyche. I was not being true to the life God had planned for me, and I suffered because of it.

Furthermore, once in the marriage, I assumed "regular" sex would take place. To my dismay, with the exception of a few times, my husband preferred oral sex. This had a profound effect on my feelings of self-worth. I felt I wasn't good enough. If I had been more of a woman, he would have wanted to have normal relations with me. One time, when we did, I became pregnant, only to have a miscarriage ten weeks later, on Columbus Day, 1990. This devastated me. I knew it was my last chance to have a baby, and I was right. The only words my husband had to say were, "The little critter didn't make it." What comforted me most were the love and support of my family and friends and the kindness of my gynecologist, Dr. Joseph Zebari, and the anesthesiologist, Dr. Chris Hines, who did my anesthesia when I had a D & C. The harder I tried to make things work, the worse matters became. My husband started to openly go out drinking and to come home late.

As a result, I became more dejected and involved myself more in work. I started working on a master's degree. What I needed was the Master's degree. Unfortunately, I was not ready to see life for what it was. I became involved with an African American man at work. At first, the relationship was platonic, more romantic than sexual. Later, it developed into a sexual relationship, thus adding to my shame. The man's wife even caught us alone together, and she subsequently pulled out two fistfuls of my hair. She had come to the school after hours and caught us in my classroom alone. At that point, nothing could stop me. I was on a downward spiral. I thought I was in love and that the feeling was mutual. Once again, the relationship was one-sided. He stayed with his wife, and I was out in the cold. I didn't realize at the time that being hypersexual was another symptom of bipolar disorder. I had started wearing shorter skirts and dresses and had gone from 135 pounds to 126 pounds. At five feet nine inches tall, that was too thin. I thought I was a hot number. My personal life, however, which was marginal at best, deteriorated more and more. Matthew Kelly says it well in *The Rhythm of Life:* "We become mad by attempting to be other than who we truly are."[2] In spite of the fact that there was mental illness on both sides of my family, I feel there was incongruence between my real self and the life I had been living. This was the impetus of my first breakdown.

A Life in Crisis

> This poor man called, and the Lord heard him; He saved him out of all his troubles.
>
> Psalm 34:6

On Friday night, March 17, 1991, I came home to Canal Fulton, Ohio loaded down with school papers and projects. I believe it was near the end of the grading period. In any case, I took a bath and then perused my closet, looking for something to wear to go out to dinner. Suddenly, I couldn't make a decision, and I couldn't reach up to the shelf to get my jeans. I kept moving back and forth, talking to myself while remaining half-dressed in my robe.

Eventually, my husband came to

see what was taking me so long, and he was surprised at my condition. I told him my mind was messed up and to take me to a local mental hospital. (I didn't know that it had been closed down.) He tried to placate me and even called my parents. At this point, I became hostile and violent, throwing the phone because he wouldn't listen to me. I knew my mind was not right. My body wouldn't function right either. I shuffled along, and my hands felt heavy.

In frustration, he took me to my parents' house in Akron. From the time we left the house, my condition worsened. Things were no better at my parents.' My aunt, Mary Kay, was visiting there. I remember clinging to her feet, begging forgiveness for anything I may have done to her. She tried to calm and told me to go lie down in my parents' bed. My parents had gone to Canal Fulton to help me, and my aunt was staying with my grandmother Starkey, who had Alzheimer's and lived with my parents. Upon my parents' return, my mother called our general practitioner, Dr. Joseph Panzner, and he said to go to the regular hospital because it had a psych ward. So my parents, my husband, and I got in my parents' station wagon and took the expressway to the hospital. I lay my head on my husband's lap and cried all the way there.

That's how I ended up at what I considered to be the best hospital in northeast Ohio. I was assigned to a great psychiatrist, Dr. Seymour Jeffries, over eighteen years ago. When my husband and my parents took me to the emergency department, I was not walking right.

When I went to sign myself in, I could barely sign my name to authorize treatment. I saw a psych resident, and he determined that I should be admitted. I was both relieved and scared, but I knew I needed help. Little did I know that I was about to begin a twelve-year journey to wellness.

The Need for Hospitalization

> For He has not despised or distained the suffering of the afflicted one; he has not hidden His face from him but has listened to his cry for help.
>
> Psalm 22:24

They kept the crisis intervention unit locked for everyone's protection. Once you were in, that was it until you were released to the stress management side. I would later describe this process as crossing over the River Jordan into the promised land.

After I was admitted and had said my goodbyes to my family, it seemed as though the people there were replicas of my family members and they were mocking me. I couldn't stand to look at them or even be around them. So I went into my room (a private room). While I was there, I heard whispering. Some man was calling my name beneath the bed. Was it the man I was interested in or my husband? I didn't want to find out. I looked down at the carpet, which had become slithering snakes!

I ran from the room, crying. A nurse in the hallway said matter-of-factly, "Sally, if you're going to cry, you have to go to your room."

I replied, "I'm not going back in that room!"

She replied, "Then we'll have to call security."

I retorted, "You can call the whole army. I'm not going back in there!"

So they called security; forced me to sit in a wheelchair; took me to isolation in the back of the hallway; and, because I was fighting, gave me a shot. That's all I remember of that night.

The next day, I heard a voice say, "Sally, I'm Dr. Jeffries."

I looked up from the mat and saw a tall, thin, bearded man seated next to me. He was young, and his face was kind. No better words had ever been spoken to me. Such was the beginning of a long and meaningful relationship. Through the upcoming years, he would see me through many peaks and many more valleys. I was diagnosed with bipolar disorder and later with obsessive-compulsive disorder. At the start, I was hospitalized frequently with an average stay of two to two and a half weeks. I would have periods of relatively good health, during which I went back to teaching.

Shortly after my first admission to the hospital, my cousins, Lisa and Jill, came to see me one evening during visiting hours. We sat at one of the tables in the day hall. They were seated on the far side near the wall, where the large windows were covered with screens, and they had a full view of the open area where patients convened. The patients obviously did not act normally. Some were talking to themselves, making weird sounds and gestures, and/or pacing. The energy was frenetic. My cousin Lisa leaned across the table to me and said, "Sally, you don't belong here."

I replied tearfully, "Yes, I do." My cousins supported me throughout my illness, but they never again visited me at the hospital. I imagine it was too disturbing for them.

In fact, very few people came to see me during my hospital stay. My parents visited every evening without fail. I eagerly awaited their visits. They were the bright spots of my day. My pastor, Reverend Gus Brown, visited often. His words of wisdom and encouragement calmed me beyond belief. My aunt, Mary Kay, came many times, as did my faithful friend, Linda, who sometimes brought her mother, Mary, or her neighbor, Lucy, who was also a teacher friend from school. The company I received during my admissions reassured me immeasurably. Without their support, I would have been like a ship lost at sea, floating in a vast ocean, not knowing where to turn.

As time went on, I continued to work obsessively. I left my husband on the Friday night before Christmas of 1991. My parents came to get some of my things, and I moved in with them. My dog, Cinnamon, whom my husband and I had given to my parents around 1988 because we couldn't housebreak her, was so glad to see me. I had thrown myself down on the bed and cried, and she came up and licked my tears away. From then on, she was devoted to me, as I was to her. While I lived with my parents, I continued to try to teach. Their emotional support was my lifeline, but it did not stop the psychosis from returning.

During my teaching years, I worked at a frantic pace. I loved the children and strived to do what was best for them. The lessons I taught were solid and meaningful. Yet I had increasing difficulty staying on top of my written lesson plans, and paper grading became insurmountable. Some of my former students helped me by grading the easier work of spelling and math. I did a lot with writing, including journals, and this was labor intensive. I took home basketfuls of work every night and on the weekends. I was exhausted most of the time.

Because of my medicines, I began to gain weight, and I noticed in photographs of myself a wild-eyed look. I struggled for a sense of normalcy. I rarely sat at my desk and kept moving throughout the day. I once taped myself in a lesson and heard my shoes clicking rapidly across the wooden floor. I was surprised at just how much I walked around and how fast I talked.

I couldn't seem to stop myself. This was yet another sign of my mania.

A good friend and colleague of mine, Murielene White, who team-taught with me, was my strongest support at school. She and I had lunch together, and we often met at Denny's on the weekends. We shared a lot about school, men, and life in general. I was devastated in July of 1999 when she was murdered by her husband, who then killed himself. She had just turned sixty-five and was looking forward to retirement. I suffered a major depression as a result.

My first principal, Barbara Whaley, was also a great support to me. She saw the good in me and was undaunted by my mental illness. She encouraged me and believed in me. When she was transferred to another building, I was greatly saddened. During her tenure, I had many breakdowns, of which she was very understanding. I made a suicide attempt in 1992, and she was supportive beyond belief.

One day, in the spring of 1992, I was looking out of my classroom window down into the parking lot. I became overwhelmed with the fear that the FBI was after me for committing heinous sexual crimes against children. When I left school, I was in a panic. I thought I had to end my life before the FBI caught up with me and exposed me for the monster I thought I was. I couldn't bear to disgrace my parents. I went to the drugstore and bought an X-acto knife and a bottle of Nytol. I had moved in to a second-story apartment not far from my parents just a short time beforehand.

I went there and went into the tub to do the deed. Right after I had stepped into the tub, the phone rang. I answered it and found out it was my principal. She was worried about me since I had left school so suddenly. She told me that my Aunt Kay and Uncle Richard, who had been visiting the school, were going to my parents' house, who were out of town in Buffalo, New York for a conference for their work at a rescue mission. My principal convinced me to go there. I put the knife and pills in my purse and went. This was just one of many examples of divine intervention.

I believe that even in my madness God was watching out for me. My principal called at just the moment I was going to cut myself. My aunt and uncle were there at the school and stayed with my class when I left. I could have been fired and never been able to get the help I needed through my benefits with Akron Public Schools. God knows the future and he can cause things to happen to bring about a chain of events according to his will. Some people ask "Why me?" "Why did God let this happen?" Sometimes God allows things to happen to us for a greater good. On my first night in the psych unit, my mom said, "Maybe some day you'll help someone else." I didn't want to hear that. I just wanted to get back to teaching. I wanted to be normal again. This was a driving force in me for years.

When I got to my parents' house, I talked with my aunt and uncle, but all the while, my mind was racing. I knew I did not feel right. I still felt the FBI was closing in on me. After I'd been there a short time, my husband (we were not yet divorced) arrived. He convinced me to go with him despite my aunt and uncle's objections. I told him I wanted to go to the hospital. He took me there and let me walk around the first floor, looking for the emergency room. We left when we couldn't find it. He took me to the two-year college where he was taking classes and left me in the library. The college was in the next county.

I tried to read, but my thoughts kept going back to the FBI. I went into the women's restroom. No one was there, so I took a whole bottle of Nytol. Then I took the stall next to the wall. I sat on the floor and cut my wrists, first the right and then the left. When I saw the blood, I immediately thought of the song "Power in the Blood" and Jesus' dying for my sins. I knew I didn't want to die. I tried to wipe my blood off the floor. Finally, I realized I needed to get help. I ran out of the library and went to the main building of the college, about five minutes away. I told the receptionist that I needed to see my husband. The blood was covered by my long-sleeved sweater. When he came down, he swore at me and asked what I wanted. I showed him what I'd done. He went back to the receptionist and told her to call an ambulance. The paramedics came in no time and took me to the closest hospital. I overheard the paramedics tell my husband in a disgusted tone that my injuries were just superficial. They were disgusted with me, I believe, for wasting their time. They acted like I did it for attention

At the hospital, they stitched my wounds and had me drink an activated charcoal drink to make me throw up. The next thing I knew my pastor, Reverend Gus Brown, was there. My mother-in-law had also come. Evidently, my husband had called them. My pastor asked both my mother-in-law and my husband to leave and said he would stay with me. My pastor contacted my parents, and they came back from New York. They were there to meet me when I was transferred by ambulance to Akron General Medical Center, where I had been previously treated.

During my stay, one of the nursing assistants named Barbara bathed me because I couldn't get my stitches wet, and she shaved my legs because I wasn't allowed a razor. Her soft, soothing voice reminded me of Pearl Bailey. She made me feel safe and secure. We developed a friendship that has lasted to this day. Barbara and another nursing assistant, Rhonda, helped keep a light, friendly atmosphere on the unit. They showed they really cared about the patients by listening and taking care of whatever needs arose.

Following my suicide attempt, I moved back in with my parents, yet I had many more psychotic breaks with reality. Each time, I would go back to teaching, but I was having difficulty doing the job I loved so much. My next principal was a man who had no understanding of mental illness. He actively tried to get rid of me. He was very negative and self-centered, a polar opposite of my first principal. One day on my way to work, I was in a car accident and had a minor concussion. During my lunch break, I went into the library and lay on the carpeted stage because my head was pounding. He came by and saw me and he went to my colleague, Murielene, and asked her if I was taking my medicine. He was constantly looking for ways to prove I was a mental case. Fortunately for me, he became superintendent of a smaller district and soon had other worries.

I got a divorce in October 1992. I don't remember a lot about it because I was in the hospital for much of it. My dad got power of attorney over me and went to court and signed all the papers. I still have a mental block for most of that time. The time I spent with my husband is like a lost decade of my life. (I dated him for six years and was married to him for 4 and a half years.) My parents helped me especially during 1992. For awhile my dad even did my checkbook. Everyday functioning was very difficult for me.

For the next three years, I tried to teach, but in between I was hospitalized nearly every six months or so. The only thing that gave me solace was to spend time with my pets and with my family. Yet I remember one time in the summer when my parents and I went out to my aunt, Mary Kay, and uncle, John's house for a sobriety party for one of my uncle, Dale's, friends. Their living room was full of people many whom I didn't know, and the only place to sit was on an ottoman in front of a chair near the kitchen. Someone motioned for me to sit there, and I thought someone was going to come up through the ottoman with a big knife and kill me. I just froze there by the kitchen. My parents ended up taking me home. I called my psychiatrist's emergency number once in the car. Dr. Moshe Torem, who often substituted for Dr. Jeffries, was on duty. The day before he had released me from the hospital and I had a prescription for Ativan (an anti-anxiety medication). He told me to take an extra pill which I did. But it ended up I had to be re-admitted to the hospital.

In January 1995, I was sitting at my desk in the front of the classroom and had a girl at the table next to me stapling papers. I only had sixteen students, yet suddenly I felt they were all coming to get me, and I panicked. I ran across the hall and asked Murielene to watch my class. I went to the office and told the new principal that I had to go home. He said that was all right, and I called my mom to come get me. When I walked out the door, I knew I'd never be back. I didn't know it then, but my beloved teaching career was at an end. I just wasn't capable anymore of working full-time as a teacher.

Bill Siegferth, the president of Akron Teacher's Association, the teacher's union was instrumental in helping me apply for disability. In addition, I had to be examined by two psychiatrists, Dr. Jeffries and another one out of the city, to confirm my diagnosis. They concurred and State Teacher's Retirement System granted my disability in April of 1995. I was very grateful for all AEA and STRS did for me at a time when I could barely function.

Life after Teaching

> The Lord himself goes before you and will be with you;
> He will never leave you nor forsake you. Do not be afraid;
> Do not be discouraged.
>
> Deuteronomy 31:8

Each day after that fateful day was a struggle. I could barely face getting out of bed to meet each day. Why bother? Without teaching, I was nothing—or so I thought. It didn't take any time at all for me to sink deeper and deeper into depression. All I did was sleep with my dog, Cinnamon, and my two cats, Butterscotch and Tawny, and drink chocolate milk. In no time, I had gained sixty pounds.

Fortunately, my teacher's disability covered 60 percent of my wages financially. And I was allowed to work outside the teaching field. I got a part-time job as a secretary at a machine shop for a few months during 1995. I had to drag myself to work every day.

Then my big break came. A good friend of mine, Tyla Brown Sherman, was opening a day care she named Wonder World Child Development Center, and she wanted me to work part-time (four to sixteen hours a week.). So, August 26, 1996, I began working as a secretary there. I worked for nine months without pay. It was a labor of love. When the daycare was bringing in more money, I was paid a lump sum for my wages. Some weeks, when my depression was worse, I could barely work four hours, yet my boss understood. She told me I could catch up when I felt up to it. There aren't many bosses who would do that. There will never be another one like her. My heart is filled with gratitude for the chance she gave me to contribute and to be around children once again.

I worked at the daycare for ten years, until November 30, 2006. During that time, I tried to work a variety of part-time jobs in addition to the day care. Usually, this only lasted for a short time (less than a year). I was working for near minimum wage, which was difficult to take, but I was thankful to be working. My psychiatrist says I'm the "workingest" patient he has.

I was not a rapid cycler going from mania to depression in short intervals. My mania and depression lasted at least two weeks. Often depression lasted for months where I spent most of my time in bed with little motivation to do anything. I felt guilty for doing so little which further added to my depression. Usually the depression would lift and I would start to feel better once the medication reached the right level in my body.

With mania, it usually started with a lack of sleep. My dad said I was very "hyper"-flitting from one thing to another. My thoughts began to race. I thought of so many things to do. I couldn't rest when it came time to sleep. I stayed up all night cleaning and organizing my things. I even got an old toothbrush and scrubbed the baseboards. When I start to get overly concerned about cleanliness, that is a sign my mania is returning.

After several nights of not sleeping, I would begin to get psychotic. I had a sense of unreality where I couldn't distinguish what was real and what wasn't. I misinterpreted people's actions and thought they were out to harm me. I became increasingly paranoid. Sometimes, though, I would find out later what I was paranoid about was true as in the case of some of the undermining things my husband was doing to me. I bought a sign some years ago that says, "Just because you're paranoid, doesn't mean they're not out to get you." It still hangs on a bulletin board in my sewing room.

When I was manic, I talked fast and louder than usual. I couldn't be still for very long. I was constantly busy. I also spent a lot of money-charging large amounts on my credit cards. For awhile, I was charging at least $30 a day on my Visa, and it didn't take long for the bills to add up. My pastor helped me budget in order to pay off my debt after I got divorced, but it wasn't long that I had charged thousands of dollars more-mostly for veterinary procedures for my pets but also for gifts for other people. While my periods of depression were a significant part of my illness, I was mostly bothered by mania. The problem with mania is that it feels so good. I felt on top of the world until I would get psychotic and eventually sink into a deep depression.

Psychosis for me was scary and confusing. I thought at the time that I was making perfect sense. My delusions seemed very real to me. I thought I was being very logical. I couldn't understand why everyone else didn't get it. I often sought out my parents during this time even going to Haven of Rest Ministries, Inc. where they worked for a reality check. The Haven of Rest is a rescue mission in Akron that provides food, clothing, and shelter for the homeless. My parents would remind me of what was real and that would help temporarily, but until I got the right level of medication in my body, I would rethink my delusion and come up with an even more bizarre one.

I remember one summer years ago when I went downtown to the Haven of Rest where my dad was setting up for the annual community picnic in the mission's parking lot. He and his coworkers were lining up and spacing tables for the people to sit at. They had the tables flat on the ground so they could get the spacing right. In my mind, I thought the tables were graves where I had buried my victims.

When I told my dad my thoughts, he reminded me that they were just tables for the picnic. Then he took me home. His words helped for awhile, but when I got home I thought of other ways I could have buried people. This type of thinking happened to me for years.

Usually, when I couldn't get the thoughts out of my mind, my parents would take me to the emergency room at Akron General and I'd be admitted. My medication would have to be adjusted. My psychiatrist would monitor my progress, or lack of it, until the medication had the proper affect. This usually took at least two weeks.

Pet Therapy

> ... and who gives food to every creature. His love endures forever.
>
> Psalms 136:25

Over the years, I acquired a number of pets. My parents very graciously accepted each new addition. I started with Cinnamon, who was a loving, loyal, orange-brown Lab mix. She followed me everywhere I went. She learned the basic commands at age eleven when I enrolled her in the "Doggie Brigade" to visit patients at the local hospitals. She was the perfect dog. I loved her more than I loved myself.

At the time of my divorce, October

1992, I was out at my aunt, Mary Kay, and uncle, John Warlop's house in Sharon Center. Their cat, Bandit, had had a litter of kittens. I picked out a small orange one and named him Tawny. When I took him to school, a fellow teacher friend of mine, Lucy Maple, a cat lover, told me I should get another to keep him company. I went back and picked out another smaller orange one and named her Butterscotch. I gave them both a bath in the sink to rid them of fleas. Later, they would both develop diabetes.

On July 26, 1997, I was going to Jo-Ann Fabrics, where I worked part-time. An orange-colored puppy ran out from under my car when I started it. She ran behind our trash dumpsters. I coaxed her out and took her inside. I showed her to my parents, and because she matched my other pets, I said it was destiny that we keep her—hence the name, Destiny. She is a medium-sized shepherd mix who the vet determined was about six months old. Matching may seem a strange reason to acquire a pet, but I've always had a thing about matching. My friend, Linda, teases me about having to match my underwear to my clothes. This may be a residual effect of my OCD. I don't know. I know I still like things orderly and organized. I feel better when things are in order, yet I am not overly concerned with cleanliness like the days when I was manic all the time. I don't seem to have any compulsion that I perform to appease my obsessions. I just like things the way I like them. I don't see anything wrong with that.

My pets have been an invaluable part of my recovery. They don't care if I'm manic or depressed or paranoid. They love me anyway. I've read that petting a pet lowers a person's blood pressure. Well, I can attest to the face that they also reduce anxiety. When I used to have night terrors, I was fearful that the devil was going to get me or that I was going to die in the night. I would lie next to my dogs and/or cats and pet them praying and sometimes crying all the while. In a little while, I'd be asleep. Sometimes when I cried one of the dogs would lick my tears away. Even now if I am getting manic and having trouble getting to sleep, I will simultaneously pet one dog with one hand and one cat with the other. I try to match my breathing with theirs, and before I know it I'm asleep.

These four pets—Cinnamon, Destiny, Tawny, and Butterscotch—stayed right with me on my bed during my depression over the loss of Murielene in 1999. Only Destiny remains of the original four. Non-cat people will say that cats don't understand people the way dogs do. But I know they do. They just show it differently.

I am basically a dog person, but cats seem to come to me. One October day in 1998, Tyla, my boss at the daycare, said she heard an animal crying outside the window. I went out and found a tiny, black kitten. When I picked him up, he hissed and spit. I told Tyla I would take him to the humane society because I already had too many pets. When I got there, the receptionist told me he was too young for them to take him. They did not have overnight staff. He was around three-weeks-old and needed to be fed every three hours. She told me what formula to buy, and I went to the pet store and bought a can and a bottle. My parents took the new addition with equanimity. They even helped with the feedings. I named him Spitfire. He lived up to his name, biting the nipple off the bottle.

After feeding Spitfire for weeks, I became attached to him. I couldn't bear to take him back to the shelter. He fit in well with the family and usually only showed his bad side when he went to the vet or if we touched his back end while petting him. When I took him to be neutered and declawed he gave the vet techs some trouble and threw himself at the front of the cage hissing all the while. He did the same thing some years later in 2004 when he had to have surgery to remove bladder stones. Dr. Frederick Keller skillfully and successfully performed the surgery. Spitfire still takes medication to stop the formation of the stones. When I first tried to give it to him, he bit and scratched me so bad I had to get a tetnus shot. But I was relentless. I didn't want to pay close to $500 for another surgery. I tried pairing the pill with a treat, and it worked. Now he asks for his pill by meowing when my dad or I come by in the morning and evening. (I gave Spitfire to my parents when I moved out because he really loves my mom.)

In the early 1990s, Linda Clark, who was the art teacher at David Hill School where I taught, invited me to her house on Friday nights to do crafts along with Lucy and some other teacher friends. I accepted her invitation, not knowing that our friendship would continue to this day. Linda has been my closest friend in Ohio. She never seems shocked by what I say. Once, when she and her mother, Mary, came to see me in the hospital, I showed her some meat I was saving in a drawer of my nightstand for the wolf that I thought was on the unit. She never told me there was no wolf on the unit. She just said, "You're trying to make friends." That's a great friend.

Linda and her husband, Jim, had three dogs: Abbey, a Gordon setter; Luka, a German short-haired pointer; and then newcomer Lily, who is a miniature dachshund. I loved going to their house. All of the dogs were friendly, but Lily liked to sit on my lap. This was my first experience with a lap dog, and I always dreamed of having one someday. Then, in December 1999, I was in the hallway of the school where my Spanish lessons were held waiting for my class to begin. I have been taking Spanish lessons since 1996. A woman named Elaine was asking my Spanish teacher, *Dra. Juanita,* if she would want a miniature dachshund. My teacher said she couldn't at that time. After that class was dismissed, I went up to Elaine and asked her if I could have the dog if it was all right with my parents. She said yes and gave me her phone number. My parents agreed, and that was how I came to get Rudy, a beautiful, two-year-old, black and tan, longhaired, miniature dachshund. The only bad habit Rudy had was he loved to chase cats. I had to put up baby gates on both sides of the living room to work on training him not to do this. Eventually, I succeeded. Rudy brought such joy into our lives.

Tragically, on Monday, March 6, 2003, Rudy suddenly became paralyzed. I took him to my vet, Dr. Anne Phlipot at West Akron Veterinary Clinic. She had cared for my other pets as well after Dr. Keller retired. Sadly, she recommended emergency surgery because he had blown a disk in his back. He was only five years old. I didn't have the money, but my dad offered to take out a loan. When I got to the hospital, however, they had a credit card plan that would give me a year to pay it off without interest. Divine intervention again! Dr. Sheldon Padgett from Metropolitan Veterinary Hospital expertly performed the surgery. The surgery was successful, but the total cost, with hospitalization and therapy, was over $2,700. I took a second job as a waitress to pay it off. I was on a new medicine (Abilify), one my doctor said was usually used for schizophrenics. I did great on it. I was working sixty hours a week. I did this for nine months, until November 2003. Then I had a major psychotic break and had to be hospitalized. That was the end of my waitressing career. But I managed to pay the loan off before the end of the year.

After Rudy came Baby, a white and gray miniature cat. She was crossing the field in front of our house in October 2000, and my dogs were barking wildly. I went out, and she seemed like she wanted me to follow her, so I did. She went over to a woodpile by a house two doors over. She let me pick her up. She was dirty, and her nose was scratched. Her one ear had no fur. She only weighed about four pounds. I remembered that the house next door had a boy who had been looking for a cat, so I went there to see if this cat might be theirs. The woman who answered the door said the cat wasn't hers. She said it had been abandoned by the people from the second house that had moved away. Of course, I took her home.

When my Dad saw her, he said, "Not another cat!" But she looked so bedraggled his heart melted. When I took her to the vet, she tested Baby, and she tested positive for feline leukemia. I was devastated. Dr. Phlipot recommended putting Baby down, but I couldn't do it. My dad built a hutch in the garage to keep her in. It took both of us to give her medicine for ear mites that she also had, plus pills for worms. What a start to life. She was only six months old.

When the weather got really cold, my dad put a screen across the doorway to half of the basement, and we kept Baby down there. My vet thought it was too risky to have her in the same house with my other cats, but I couldn't leave her in the cold. I kept the other cats upstairs. In six months, I had her retested for feline leukemia. She tested negative! I was so happy. She could now really be part of the family.

Baby was a sweet, little cat. She meowed for me to feed her first thing when I got up. If I tried to drink my coffee first, she would nudge my hand, spilling coffee all over. She trained me to feed her first. Baby lived for seven years before getting lymphoma, a blood cancer. She was on prednisone and seemed to improve. However, after about a month, she stopped eating and died a couple days later. After that, I couldn't drink my first cup of coffee without thinking of her.

My pets have given me such joy and love. They make life worth living. I had a suicidal thought when Rudy was dying. I thought I couldn't go on without him. I remembered feeling the same way when I had to put Cinnamon to sleep at fourteen, due to a severe kidney infection that was resistant to even the strongest antibiotic. But the love of my other pets carried me through. I knew I needed to care for them. They needed me, and I needed them. They are always there for me. Not a day goes by that I don't pet or hold each one. Their lives are precious, and I am grateful to God for giving them to me and for allowing me the means to care for them. I am grateful to the doctors and staff at West Akron Veterinary Clinic for keeping them in good health, for tending to their ailments, and for helping to end their suffering when that time comes. The support they have given to me in all of these times, good and bad, has been invaluable. The receptionist, Sue Ringler, gives me practically daily advice about my pets. She has become a good friend. Sue helped me keep tabs on whether I was getting manic or not. I would ask her whether she thought I was and usually she would tell me "No." If I was getting overly paranoid about some symptoms I'd noticed with my pets, she would explain the possibilities in a way that comforted me yet let me know if there was something I had to keep an eye on.

The thing that makes West Akron Veterinary Clinic so special is that they make each client feel as if they are the only client even though they have hundreds of clients. They treat the pets the same way and they remember them all. They send sympathy cards when a pet dies and all the staff writes a note and signs them. One doesn't find that personal touch often in business. It is a treasure when one does.

Human Support System

> Therefore encourage one another and build each other up, just as in fact you are doing.
>
> I Thessalonians 5:11

I have been blessed with a marvelous support system. My family and friends have always been there for me. They have loved and accepted me, even when I did bizarre things. They hurt when I did. They understood when I was confused and irrational. Most of all, they listened to me, which showed they cared more than anything.

My parents, above all, never failed me. They no doubt prayed for my healing, but they were undaunted by anything I did. They saw the best in me. I am sure they had untold sorrow at my condition, but they never complained. They just waited patiently for the good times to come. They weathered the storms right along side of me.

My grandmother, Starkey, who lived with my parents was a great storyteller. I loved to talk to her about her days in Eckhart, Maryland where she grew up. She had so many funny stories of the pranks she and her friends played on people especially during Halloween. Before I got married, she and I had our bedrooms next to each other and my parents slept in a bedroom in the basement. I spent a good deal of time in her bedroom reminiscing. Around the time I got sick, my grandmother fell a number of times. My parents had to call the paramedics because they couldn't get her up because she was too heavy for them to lift. Consequently, she had to go to a nursing home. My husband and I visited her there often. Because of her Alzheimer's she had forgotten a lot, but I remember the last time I saw her she turned in her wheelchair and said, "I love you, Sally." She developed pneumonia and died on October 18, 1991 just a few months before I left my husband. She was eighty years old.

My grandmother, Nitz, came over to my parents' house frequently. She and I became closer when I lived with her when I first came to Akron and I worked at First National Bank. She used to make me Cream of Wheat every morning. It was the perfect start to the day. Both of my grandmothers had sayings they always said which still come to my mind years after their deaths. My grandma, Nitz, used to say, "If it's not one thing, it's another;" "It's always something;" and "You gotta keep a goin.'" She had a lot of energy and looked years younger than she was. When we'd go to the grocery store, she would ask the cashier, "How old do you think I am?" The cashier would always guess younger, and that gave my grandma a thrill. She also suffered from depression from time to time and would become moody. My dad remembers when he was growing up she would spend a lot of time in her bedroom when she was depressed, and his father would tell him and his five brothers and sisters not to bother her. She spent her last years in a nursing home as well. She got a blood infection and died a prolonged death at the age of ninety-four. That was November 22, 1999.

My aunt, Liz, one of my dad's older sisters, developed bipolar disorder at a young age. The onset was partially due to her miscarriage of twin boys and a failed marriage which was similar to what I had experienced. She spent many years in an institution and suffered with the disease for the rest of her life. She understood my plight probably better than anyone. She cared deeply about my progress. She wept with me when I was sick and celebrated with me when I was well. She really loved my little dachshund Rudy.

My dad and I would take Rudy to the nursing home to see her, and he brightened her day.

She died in that nursing home on January 8, 2006 at the age of seventy which was her sister, Kathleen's, birthday. I sorely miss both of my grandmothers and my aunt, Liz.

Richard and Kathleen McDowell, my dad's other older sister and her husband, offered their support from Wadsworth, Ohio. They were interested in my progress as were their children Alan and Susan and their families. They stayed in touch even after they moved out-of-state.

My aunt, Mary Kay Warlop, is my mom's younger sister. She has been like my second mother. She and my uncle, John, opened their home to me. I felt comfortable there. I knew I could go to them with any problem. I didn't have to ask for their support. It was understood. Their children Lisa, Jill, and Johnny have always been more like siblings than cousins. They and their families accepted me as I was, but most of all, they loved me.

My uncle, Dale Starkey, is my mom's younger brother. He had my grandmother Starkey's knack for telling funny stories. I could always count on him to make me laugh.

Many of his stories were from his drinking days in his youth. He got sober on November 5, 1983 which was the day my cousin Lisa had her daughter Tara. He had gone to the hospital when he was drunk and was asked to leave. This was his big wake-up call. He went into treatment six days later. He affectionately calls Tara his sobriety baby. He knows what it's like to reach bottom and climb up. He is grateful for what God has done for him and he shares it lovingly with others.

My younger brother, Daryl, offered his support from Chicago. Although I usually only saw him at Christmastime, he brought thoughtful gifts for me which showed he cared. When we were growing up, we argued a lot, but when we got in trouble, we stuck together. He was the first one I called when I was afraid of my husband right before the Christmas of 1991. Daryl convinced me to call my parents so they could come get me in Canal Fulton.

My good friend, Deborah Klemm Vogel, who was my first (and last) college roommate, offered her support from Michigan through timely cards, letters, gifts, and e-mails. She knew me well and always had just the right words of encouragement. She felt my pain. My friend since fifth grade, Pam Link Dobberstein, wrote letters and sent cards from Illinois. She never forgot to send presents on my birthday and at Christmas. Locally, Linda helped me stay balanced by always lending a listening ear and offering wise counsel. She knows me better than just about anyone, except my parents and my aunt, Mary Kay.

My Spanish teachers, *Dra. Juanita Lijerón* and *Manena Vidlak,* have given me unfailing moral support and encouragement through the years. *Juanita* has known me since I was critically ill. Even after she moved to Florida, she kept in touch. She recommended *Manena* to me, and it was a perfect fit. I started out in group lessons with *Manena* in August 2001, but people have dropped out over the years, so the group lessons turned into private ones. Since that time, we have become closer, and I seek her counsel whenever I make a major decision. She has never failed me.

Manena is Catholic and originally from Argentina. Our difference in religions was never an issue for us because we both have a great love for Jesus. There was a time when I was really bothered by the devil. Some of my friends tried to tell me there was no devil, but having been psychotic and seen his emissary in a dream, I was sure there was. Instead of trying to dissuade me *Manena* gave me a Spanish warfare prayer to ward off the devil. I still have it on the mirror of my dresser. It really helped me. It goes:

Al Diablo

(To the Devil)

Te quito todo poder sobre mi.
(I take away all your power over me.)
Ningun poder puede afectarme;
(No power can affect me;)
Ni mi vida;
(Nor my life;)
Ni mi ambiente;
(Nor my environment;)
Ni mi hogar;
(Nor my home;)

Ni mi familia.
(Nor my family.)

Working on my master's degree took all of my effort in the early to mid-nineties. I battled depression and often had trouble focusing. I often fell asleep in the study carrel at the University of Akron's library while I was doing research. This was in the days before personal computers and the Internet were in vogue. I copied articles from educational journals, highlighted them, and took notes by hand. It was very labor intensive.

Writing my thesis was the single most difficult task I'd ever undertaken. My mentor and advisor was Dr. Ralph Darr. I'd had Dr. Darr as a professor as an undergraduate in "Human Development and Learning" and in "Behavioral Bases," a core graduate level course in the Department of Education. It was a fascinating course in human behavior. Dr. Darr was an engaging lecturer. He had a wry sense of humor which I liked, and he was kind. I found the course to be challenging, and informative.

As a thesis advisor, Dr. Darr was encouraging and patient. He understood the difficulties I was having and he guided me every step of the way. He praised my writing abilities and suggested that I try and get published in an educational journal. But all of my efforts were on finishing my thesis. I focused on studying coherence in children's journal writing as this was of great interest to me.

My thesis was entitled: "Daily Journal Assessment: Examining Factors Affecting Coherence." I took a sample of writing from my colleague, Murielene White's, second-grade class and measured how many sentences adhered to the topic and whether spelling affected coherence. Then I did a statistical analysis of the findings. I found 90% of the students' sentences in the journal entries contributed to the topic which indicated that the second-grade students sampled could write meaningful entries. Little correlation was found between spelling errors and coherence.

I graduated summa cum laude in May of 1996 a little over a year since I went on disability. Unfortunately, after I graduated, I was not mentally fit enough to work in an area that used my teaching skills. Under the terms of my disability, I couldn't do any job related to teaching even part-time.

I don't regret getting an advanced degree, however, because I use many of the skills I honed in the process-skills such as writing, analyzing, organizing, and planning. All of these helped me in writing this book and in planning for the future.

In addition, I met Dr. Darr's wife, Alice, who was also a professor but at Kent State University. Both remain my friends today. They are supportive of my endeavors and are happy with and for me in my accomplishments. Both are retired from education now, and we don't see each other often, but when we do, it's just like old times. That's the sign of true friendship. I know they are always in my corner.

Reverend Curt Thomas and his wife, Eileen, the former directors of Haven of Rest Ministries, have supported me since I came to know them when my mom first started at the mission when my parents moved back to Ohio from Illinois, where I grew up.

My mom was hired in the summer of 1982 as a housemother for Harvest Home, the women's building. She worked there for almost twenty-three years, retiring in June of 2005. She was well-loved for her outgoing personality and respected for her no-nonsense approach to discipline. She was known as "the hugger" since she freely offered hugs to those she met. For many years, I helped her at Christmastime get gifts together from the donations for the residents and former residents. It was almost an insurmountable task, but we had fun doing it together.

My dad was hired a couple of years later in 1984 as the facilities manager. He holds that position today. He is seventy-years-old and still does a great job. He has a vast amount of knowledge about carpentry, plumbing, and electrical work. I worked for him at the mission doing cleaning and outside work during the summers while I was teaching. He was as understanding a boss as he was a father. He took time to explain things clearly. If that didn't work, his favorite words were, "Let me show you." He had been an elementary school teacher for eleven years in Illinois, and he has the heart of a teacher still.

I helped out at the mission part-time, doing an assortment of jobs from the summer of 1985 until the

Christmas of 2000. The staff, then and now, have been loving and kind to me as they are with the clients who seek refuge. They do an invaluable service to the community. They are dedicated to serving God and furthering His kingdom.

In addition to my family and friends, God has brought into my life many knowledgeable medical professionals, whom I consider friends. My general practitioner, Dr. Panzner, has been my doctor since 1981, shortly after I came to Akron. He had the foresight to send me to Dr. Jeffries at the outset. His expert, sensitive care brought me through many turbulent times. During most of the years that I was sick, I looked at him as a near deity. I didn't make a major decision without consulting him. I didn't trust my own judgment because I had made so many poor choices in the past. I knew I was getting better when I started making decisions without checking with Dr. Jeffries or my parents first.

Dr. Jeffries and Dr. Panzner both concurred to send me to an outstanding nephrologist, Dr. Susan Ray, in 2001when my kidneys started to fail due to the lithium I was taking. Thanks to her help, my kidney function has improved and is now stabilized. She also detected my high blood pressure a few years ago and worked with Dr. Panzner to get me on the proper medication.

The nurses at the hospital gave me outstanding care. They were kind and compassionate. Even at my most psychotic, they treated me as if I was normal. They didn't talk down to me. They told me about themselves, which not only humanized them; it humanized me. Leslie, a nurse who was obviously pregnant, told me about her plans for her baby. Years later, after she had left the hospital to raise her children, I met her in the emergency department waiting room. Her son was then fourteen. We chatted like old friends. Bekke, also a nurse, once told me about her dogs, and we shared stories. Later, I would become even better friends with her.

Other nurses influenced me by their manners. On the more critical unit, Vince always had a smile and often a joke. Linda was energetic and positive. Her enthusiasm was contagious. Claudia was quiet and thoughtful. She had the patients' best interests at heart. Grace was soothing. She spoke softly, but her words were powerful. Jaimie was quiet and kind. He was sensitive to the patients' feelings and explained things patiently. Rae had a quiet, unassuming strength and was very loving.

On the less acute unit, Diane was friendly and concerned. She patiently took time to listen to my concerns. Cathy was thorough and businesslike but had a heart of gold. Kathy was bubbly and positive. She never seemed to have a bad day. Joyce was friendly and caring. She took time to talk, and I felt like I was her only patient even though I knew she was busy with others. Paul was quiet and sensitive. He had a wry sense of humor. Pat was loving and kind. She radiated joy. Jeff was conscientious and sincere. He paid attention to what I told him. Even if it was delusional, he would gently remind me of reality in a way that was not condescending. He seemed to understand my struggle and was empathetic. Often, at night, I couldn't sleep and would walk the halls even though the rules were that the patients were to be in one's own room at night. Instead of chastising me, Helen, one of the night nurses, would suggest warm milk before I returned to bed. One night, I went to the section of the hallway outside the nurses' station where there was a fish tank and sat down on the floor. When Ed, one of the other night nurses, saw me, he came out and told me I'd have to go back to bed. I told him it was my job to watch the fish. He patiently told me I'd have to do that in the morning, and he walked me back to my room.

Part of the therapy in the hospital was for the patients to go to various classes. The first group of the morning was goals group. Duane usually conducted this in the day hall after breakfast. He went over the events from the newspaper and helped the patients plan their days. The second class was occupational therapy, which started at 9:00 a.m. Becky was the group leader. She was positive and upbeat. On all of my sedating medications, I often wondered how anyone could be so perky in the morning. Still, I loved OT. We got to make trivets made with ceramic tile and grout on a wooden or metal base. This improved our concentration and planning skills. We also did other interesting crafts involving painting, staining, sewing, and gluing to make useful items. The class ended promptly in one hour. I always wished it could go longer.

There were other classes such as: goals; anger management; time management; managing stress; group therapy; recreational therapy; and, my favorite, art therapy. Heidi was the art therapist. She developed lessons that used artistic mediums to express feelings. She often read stories to go along with the project of the day. We made masks, sculpted, painted, and drew pictures. We used all kinds of paper and drawing materials: oil pastels, markers, watercolor, tempera, glitter glue, and paint. The lessons were all very creative, and I enjoyed them immensely. They helped me to express my feelings and often revealed feelings I didn't know I'd had. The activity where we made masks reflected this especially. We were to paint on the outside of the mask how we presented ourselves to the world and on the inside how we feel inside. I painted a bright happy almost clownish face on the outside but the inside was dark and brooding. I hadn't realized there was such a dichotomy between my real self and the one I showed to others. I was laughing on the outside and crying on the inside. This particular lesson facilitated my coming to that conclusion and dealing with it.

All the rest of the staff on the psychiatric units also gave a personal touch to their work, which helped the patients feel at home in a very foreign environment. The unit clerks were the ward secretaries. They helped the units stay organized and greeted patients and family members. They answered the phones as well as the questions of the patients. Two unit clerks that I most remember were Nancy and Susan. Both were friendly and approachable. They weren't put off by my questions or requests, even though they were busy keeping the patients' charts up-to-date, along with a host of other duties. When I asked a question, they looked me in the eye and stopped what they were doing. I really felt they cared about me. One of the best things I remember them doing for me is offering me a steno notebook to write my thoughts in when I asked for paper. The notebooks helped me record my thoughts in an orderly fashion. I wrote down things I wanted to ask Dr. Jeffries when he came in for his daily, morning visits. Before that time, I would often forget things I wanted to ask because my mind was racing with so many thoughts.

In the evenings, after visiting hours were over, we had recreational therapy. Deb, the recreational therapist, picked interesting things for us to do. We played various games which helped us get in touch with our feelings. We would discuss how we use recreation to help us unwind. This was helpful for me because I was the type of person who felt guilty for wasting time. I had a hard time unwinding. The most relaxation I did at home when I was married was to listen to music while I sewed or cleaned. It wasn't until I moved back with my parents that I did things for fun. My dad and I often took the dogs and went for long walks in the metro parks. I did go to movies a lot with my husband. Most of them were "R" rated with a lot of violence and sex. I really didn't enjoy them, but I went because my husband wanted to. When I would try and voice my dislike of a particular film, my husband would say, "It's just a movie." But the movies affected me greatly. I became less trusting of others-more paranoid that something bad was going to happen to me. Also, I started swearing when I got mad. One time in group therapy, I let loose with some expletives about something I was mad about. Later a woman in the group told me it was like listening to Snow White talk like a truck driver. I was not proud of it. In recreational therapy, however, we watched funny, wholesome movies which I enjoyed. The staff made popcorn for us as well. I still don't usually go to "R" rated movies. Whenever I've made an exception, I've regretted it.

The social workers, Russ, Kathy and Jerry, worked diligently behind the scenes to help the patients plan for their lives upon discharge from the hospital. They were part of the treatment team working together with the doctors and nurses to provide continuity of care for the patients. They also provided supportive counseling and acted as liaisons to various community resources. In addition, they helped with aftercare appointments. They were all conscientious and dedicated. I didn't have a lot of contact with them when I was a patient because I had good insurance, reasonable income, and a stable home life. But I came to know later how much they helped people without insurance, housing, and/or income. In fact, much of what they did for me I was unaware of at the time. But I remember their kindness to me and their efficiency.

Akron General also had an outpatient program called partial hospitalization. Here, the patients came during the day for group therapy and various classes. I attended partial hospitalization a number of times. I found it hard to stay awake all day, as I was on some sedating medications. However, the staff I remember was very kind to me. I learned a lot about myself during group therapy, which was the first class of the day. It was run by Larry, who was an expert in bringing out one's hidden agendas and exploring them. Nancy, the art therapist, was kind and gentle. Her soft voice soothed me. In fact, the lessons also soothed my spirit. Her lessons touched me on a deep level. We used similar mediums as we did on the unit. My favorite was drawing with oil pastels. The way the pastel glided across the paper in a smooth way and the colors blended together was comforting to me. I found my creativity to be emerging. I hadn't felt like that since I took art in junior high and had a degree of success in it. Art therapy helped me to express my feelings in color with various shadings just like my emotions. When I was depressed, my drawings were darker and more somber. When I was manic, they were bright and lively. Seeing the differences in my artwork helped me to take stock of my emotions and analyze them. I also remember doing a sculpture of my dog Destiny. Molding the material and making something dear to my heart helped me express myself. I always looked forward to art therapy, which was toward the end of the day. There were other classes, but these are the two I remember most. I also remember the kindness of the director of PH, Chris.

Photos

Sculpture entitled "Serenity" by former Art Therapist at Akron General Medical Center, Heidi Larew, NCC, PCC-S, LICDC, ATR-BC. This sculpture depicts what Sally thinks of herself as a work in progress–the happy emerging and the sad falling away.

Sally with her grandmother Elsie Nitz. Sally gave this trivet she made in Occupational Therapy to her grandmother for her birthday in July 1992.

Sally and her beloved dog, Cinnamon, in December 1996.

Sally with Rudy, Cinnamon, Butterscotch, Tawny, Spitfire, and Destiny (left to right) in December 2000. Courtesy of Quick Photo.

Sally with Destiny, Spitfire, Baby, Buttercup (back) and Nugget, and Codie (front) (left to right) in December 2006.

Part of Sally's support system: her uncle and aunt, John and Mary Kay Warlop, her uncle, Dale Starkey, and her parents, Donna and Albert Nitz (left to right) in September 2007.

Sally (center) and her ever-supportive parents Donna and Albert Nitz (left to right) in December 2007.

Sally and her current pet family: Codie, Buttercup, Sugar Pie, Nugget, Provi, and Destiny (left to right) in November 2009. Courtesy of Lyons Photography.

Everyday Living

> You will keep in perfect peace
> him whose mind is steadfast,
> because he trusts in you.
> Trust in the Lord forever,
> for the Lord, the Lord,
> is the Rock eternal.
>
> Isaiah 26:3–4

Sometimes life is a struggle between sanity and insanity. It's a fine line. I praise God for the medications that keep my mind in balance. When I thought I could cut back on my meds to stretch them out for a longer period of time, I had problems and started to get paranoid or had delusions. What I notice mostly when I take less than the prescribed dose of medication is that I start to have very bizarre dreams almost like I am dreaming while I am awake. It is very frightening because I feel on the verge of reality and unreality. Usually the next day I go back to the prescribed amount. So I know that I need the medications, regardless of what some people might think.

There are those who think, in their ignorance, that one only has to rely on God to gain strength and good health. I don't discount His influence, but I have experienced the effects of medication firsthand, and I know when it works and when it doesn't. When it's working, my faith in God is strong, and my self-esteem is intact. It's a beautiful thing. I believe it takes all three components for solid mental health.

It's amazing when the chemical imbalance begins and the mind malfunctions. Reality and unreality mix in a twisted blend. Yet, to me, everything at that time seemed real—even my paranoid delusions.

One common thought I have had is that I've committed some heinous sexual crimes against children. Working in an inner-city daycare provided the background for the obsession to occur. Consequently, I had once feared that all the African Americans in Akron were out to kill me. At that time, I even thought of pulling out in traffic to get it over with quickly. Even though I loved the children and most of the workers at the daycare where I worked, negative thoughts still came to me. During one episode, I felt that there was a sting operation in effect, and everyone at the daycare was out to get me. During this time of paranoia, I heard the voices of the workers in the hall. Their laughter rang in my ears. These thought processes are so irrational and unfathomable, yet it seemed so real at the time that it caused a panic attack.

That day, the thoughts began suddenly. I was frozen in place at my desk while using the adding machine. Each click increased my heart rate. My boss was at her desk in the same room. I thought, *She knows I'm a pedophile. She's waiting for me to make a move. Why doesn't she call her husband* [a police officer] *to blow my head off?* Time seemed to stand still. My heart was pounding, and I couldn't finish adding up the numbers. I sat at my desk awhile. Then, as quickly as the thoughts came, they faded away. I was able to finish the day's work.

My doctor says that I think thoughts of being a pedophile because I'm taking what I think is the worst possible thing and putting it on myself. This explains my connection with African Americans. Ever since reading *Roots* and watching the television series when I was in high school, I've had an affinity to African Americans and their culture. I see crimes against African Americans (such as the Atlanta child murders) as atrocities and put it on myself. I saw myself as a vile criminal and nothing could be further from the truth. Yet my self-esteem was so low at that time that I had trouble seeing the good in myself. Other people would tell me positive things about myself, but somehow I couldn't internalize it. Working with the children at the daycare helped me because, in talking to them, I realized I could never have done the things I had been thinking of. I loved the children there as if they had been my own.

When I got divorced, the Baptist church I went to was not very forgiving. Many people in the all Caucasian congregation shunned me because I had had an affair with an African American man. Thankfully, I found acceptance and solace in a predominately African American church: Akron Alliance Fellowship. The people there were loving and kind. They did not judge me for my adultery or my mental illness. They welcomed me with open arms. In fact, my Sunday school teacher, Ernie Calhoun, told me one Sunday that God forgives our sins as far as the East is from the West. This was a great comfort to me. It lifted a burden from my heart. I was greatly blessed by the love and encouragement I receive from my pastor; his wife, Elaine; and his family. His oldest daughter is my boss at the daycare (I went back in May 2007), and she is like a sister to me. We've shared many hard times together and have grown closer with each passing year. She gave me a job when no one else would take a chance on someone with a history of mental illness. For that, I will be eternally grateful.

Combating Episodes

> He gives strength to the weary and increases the power of the weak.
>
> Isaiah 40:29

Sometimes, an episode will subside with time, but usually it requires the intervention of medicine. When they become increasingly more bizarre and debilitating, they require hospitalization. The break with reality becomes too great, and functioning normally becomes impossible.

More often than not, I can tell when I need hospitalization. It's usually necessary to go through the emergency room because it usually occurs after business hours. While in the hospital, getting better requires getting the right chemical balance as well as rest and proper nutrition for the body.

From March 1991 to November 2003, I had been hospitalized fourteen times. It used to take over two weeks for me to get stabilized. Now, after having the illness so long and knowing my body better, the last few times only took four days.

At first, the other patients in the hospital seemed strange. They seemed to be mocking me or being hostile toward me. I avoided them and kept to myself. As time went on, I began to reach out to them and started treating them as individuals. By talking to them and not fearing them, I became more open to them. Consequently, I felt more like myself. Once, I started to show an illiterate man how he could make a dictionary of new words he wanted to learn and thus improve his reading skills. He was very appreciative. I found out later that he was a criminal, yet I had no fear of him. Some people judge criminals or think of them as bad or undeserving of mercy. This is especially true of murderers and rapists. I didn't know what this man's crime was. I only knew he was struggling like I was to get better. Little did I know then that I would later commit some criminal acts myself all based on delusions. By the grace of God, I was never arrested.

One delusion I had when I couldn't sleep occurred in the hospital day room one night. There was a ping-pong table there where the men and a nursing assistant were playing ping pong. I thought that the men were going to gang rape me and then cut me up with a chain saw. Then they would put me in a garbage bag and throw me out the window, saying, "There's the white trash." I remember being afraid and going to my room. Usually when I had a weird thought, I would tell my nurse and he or she would explain things to me. But this time, I hid in my room. The delusion must have passed because I don't recall the thought carrying over to the next day.

During that same time period, I tried to smother my hospital roommate with a pillow. I thought she was mocking my dead grandmother's snoring. I also thought that my lover from school wanted me to kill her as a rite of passage. I saw, through the window, my lover dancing a satanic dance on the rooftop of a building across the street. This, I interpreted as a sort of sign to kill my roommate. Fortunately, the nurses came in and caught me in the act. Then, once again, I was put in isolation.

Early in my illness, I had an episode where I told my parents that I was going to do a show at the school where I taught. My brother, Daryl, is a cabaret singer in Chicago, and maybe this is where I got the idea. Anyway, he and his friend, Gary, were visiting for Christmas, and I got it into my mind one evening that I was going to do a Whitney Houston show at school. I packed a bag, got my MacGyver boots on, and headed out the door. They tried to stop me, and I fought them. They ended up calling the paramedics to take me to the hospital because I was becoming increasingly irrational.

By the time the paramedics got there, my brother and my dad had pinned me down in the front yard. When I saw the paramedics, I thought they were part of a plan instigated by my husband to take me into a prostitution ring and pass me around. I fought all the more. While they had me down, I yelled an obscenity. They managed to strap me down and took me to the hospital by ambulance.

Once at the hospital, I was given a room by myself. I started thinking I was a squirrel and took off all of my clothes. Then I perched on the top of the bed, making chattering noises and wetting the bed, saying I was going on my husband. At that moment, a male nurse named Dave came into the room and asked me why I had taken off my clothes. I told him I was a squirrel and that I had wet the bed. He gave me my clothes and told me to put them on while he went out; when he came back he cleaned up and remade the bed.

I ended up in isolation again. There, I tried to get out of the locked room by somersaulting across the mat into the door. Eventually, I fell asleep, exhausted. My doctor said that he thought I thought I was becoming a squirrel because my husband had caught a squirrel in a box and I felt like that squirrel, trapped and put down.

Criminal at Large

> Do not hide your face from your servant; answer me quickly, for I am in trouble. Come near me and rescue me because of my foes. You know how I am Scorned, disgraced and shamed; All my enemies are before you.
>
> Psalm 69:17–19

Another time when I had a delusion and broke the law was when I stole my neighbor's truck. I was thinking that my mom had sexually abused me when I was a child. Seeing my mom cleaning a tub on her job earlier that day had prompted the idea. I thought she had cleaned my genitals with cleanser and had done untold atrocities to me like in the book *Sybil.*

I had been mulling over the possibility all day. While swimming in our backyard pool, my aunt, Mary Kay, came in and said, "Brace yourself, Effie," before she jumped in. (This was a misquoted sexual connotation from the movie "Mrs. Doubtfire.")[1] I thought, *She's in on it too.*

I got out of the pool and went into the house, preparing to leave. I wanted to go to the hospital to find Dr. Torem who gave Sodium Pentothol treatments. I had to find out if what I was thinking was true. Dr. Torem taught me to write positive things about myself called affirmations which helped me greatly. I carried them in my organizer for years. He told me to repeat them to myself four times a day-at mealtimes and at bedtime. I did this religiously because I liked and trusted him. He also told me to listen to a news radio station to focus on and analyze current events. This helped me to stay in reality and deal with it.

I got my beloved dog, Cinnamon, and a bag of dog food and took off down our long driveway. My dad had borrowed my car, so I started walking. Then I saw an old, light blue pickup truck that the migrant workers had left in the field next to our property. Thinking again of MacGyver, I checked inside, and, behold, the keys were in it. It was destiny. I loaded my dog and the food. Then I got in and started it up. I drove across the field, past a group of migrant workers, and out onto the road. I was on my way to the hospital.

When I got there, I parked in front and walked in, still barefoot and in my bathing suit, with my dog in tow. I went up to the fifth floor where Dr. Torem had his office. When I couldn't find him, I again thought of MacGyver and headed for the stairwell, trying to get to the helicopter pad. Climbing on the handrail on the top floor stairwell, I used Cinnamon's collar to try and get the sprinkler system to work and thus open the locked door. This plan did not work, so I returned to the elevator on the fifth floor.

My dog would not go into the elevator, so I headed back to the stairs. It was here I met security. One of the officers, Joel, I knew from before on the psych unit. He told me I couldn't have my dog in the hospital. They took me to emergency in a wheelchair and took Cinnamon to the parking booth for someone to pick up.

In emergency, they asked me for the keys to move my truck, at which point I told them it wasn't exactly my truck. I told them it was my neighbor's. They called my neighbor, and he said he would not press charges. But the police came and took my picture. I wrote my neighbor a heartfelt apology and thank-you note after I was admitted.

I waited to be admitted in the emergency room corridor. By this time, my parents had been called. They and my aunt had come down, but I refused to see them. I still irrationally thought that they had abused me. While waiting, I examined the three gold rings on my fingers and decided that wearing them would make me a whore. I threw them all away in a nearby trashcan: one was my class ring, one was my mother's class ring, and the other was my birthstone. They were never recovered.

After being admitted, I had a chance to talk to my doctor. He convinced me that I was not abused and that, furthermore, if I did not live with my parents, I would become a ward of the state. This convinced me to apologize to my parents. They were very understanding, considering what I had accused them of. I couldn't believe they would even speak to me, much less forgive me, but they did.

My doctor said that I was running from the idea of having mental illness. I was trying to find an explanation for it. I guess he was right. I can hardly believe I ran for over twelve years. Yet, acceptance is difficult. Gratefully, I am on the road to find it.

This was, by far, my worst episode. Yet, as I look back, it was the funniest. It is amazing to see what havoc the mind can play.

In 2001, after we had moved to another house, I broke the law again. I was thinking that I just had to get away from my parents and then everything would be all right. While my parents were sleeping, I took my 1990 Grand Am and loaded up all of my pets: three dogs and three cats. I drove on the expressway toward Cleveland, thinking I would go to my friend Deb's house in Michigan. When I called her from my cell phone, however, she did not sound like she thought it would be a good idea. I hung up the phone on her and continued driving. My next thought was to go to Yorkshire, where James Herriot was from, but I wasn't sure I could take all my pets on the plane. I got off the expressway on Route 82 and started down the road. I was thinking that maybe the man I had an affair with was out there someplace waiting for me. Then I heard, "I'll Make Love to You," by Boyz II Men on the radio, and I pulled into a drive of a house that was for sale. I thought my lover awaited me inside. I tried the back door, and it was open. I went upstairs, calling his name, but he wasn't there. Dejected and fearful that I was in a house without permission and might have left fingerprints, I left, wiping my fingerprints off the doorknob.

Next, I realized that I had left without a litter box, so I drove up the street where I had seen a drugstore. I charged a litter box, litter, a CD player, and some other things on my new credit card. While I was in the store, it seemed that no one was looking at me. All I saw were the back of people's heads. Then, when I went to the car, I thought I saw my friend from Michigan's dad in the car next to me. Maybe that was a sign. I drove down the road and stopped at a fast-food restaurant to eat. My car stalled, and two young men pushed me and the car started. I drove to a nearby motel and asked if they took pets. When they did, I charged a night's stay.

While trying to get all of the pets into the motel, one of my pets, Spitfire, escaped and ran under a parked semi. I tried to get him, but he ran away from me every time I got close. I finished putting the rest of the pets in the room and then tried again. No luck. Then I tried putting some food out by the door. Soon, he came to eat, and I managed to get him. It makes me sick to think I could have lost him because of my folly.

Later, in the room, when we were going to sleep, someone passed by the room, and Rudy, my long-haired miniature dachshund, barked. He kept barking at every noise, and I thought we were going to get kicked out. At this point, I felt desperate, and I called my parents. Even though it was the middle of the night, they answered right away. I told them what had happened and where I was. They said they would be there to get me. They saved the day. I felt like a fool. My doctor said I was still running from the fact that I had a mental illness.

Dr. Jeffries asked me if I could promise him that I wouldn't go on any more "road trips." I promised I wouldn't, and I kept that promise. When I had attempted suicide, I also promised him I wouldn't hurt myself, and I didn't.

I don't know when it was exactly that I did accept the fact that I have a mental illness, but I did. I was just determined to go back to teaching. The fact that I was probably never going to do that was harder to accept. That is probably the reason why I keep my teaching certificate-hoping one day to return.

Because of the way bipolar people are portrayed in the media-they have usually killed a child or other loved one or shot up their workplace-I started to worry that I would kill my parents in the night. I remember one night, after we had moved to our new house, I lay in bed thinking about it. I ran upstairs to my parents' room where they were sleeping. I woke them up and asked them to put away all the knives in the kitchen and lock their bedroom door. They told me they weren't locking their door, and I wasn't going to kill them, and to go back to bed. That was it. Their faith in me comforted me. I went back downstairs and went to sleep praying they were right.

Day-to-Day Living

> Never will I leave you; never will I forsake you.
>
> Hebrews 13:5

On Tuesday, August 26, 2003, insanity fell over me like a cloud. I was getting dressed for work at my second job as a waitress. I came across my dad in the basement where I had my bedroom, and he was cleaning up some sawdust from a drilling project he was working on. I thought, *All the messes he's making in the house now. He's trying to drive me crazy!* I had an unreal feeling permeating my thinking. I had a hard time getting ready. I had to wash my feet (because they smelled to me) even though I had only twenty minutes to get to the restaurant.

I fought the fear of going to work and forced myself to go. Once there, I seemed okay. I stayed busy from 4:00 p.m. until 8:00 p.m., when we closed. Waiting on customers and talking to people helped me keep my mind on others and off myself. I would suggest this to others suffering from mental illness—get out among people, stay busy, and take your medication.

While closing the restaurant, however, thoughts started to creep back in. The closer it came to 9:30 p.m., when I was due for my medication, the worse it became. I was able to finish my shift by 10:00 p.m. without anyone knowing anything was wrong but me.

My mom was waiting up for me when I got home. I took my medicine: 10 mg of Zyprexa and 5 mg of Abilify. Then I talked with her about my feelings. She is always a good sounding board. She is never shocked by what I'm thinking, and I can be completely honest with her.

I went to bed shortly afterward, but instead of subsiding, the thoughts became more bizarre. Now I was thinking that I had abused busboys and girls at the restaurant in the past, along with my other imagined past sexual crimes. *How they must hate me,* I thought. Next, I thought that a crowd of people were coming to get me and take me to the restaurant to rape and kill me in front of an audience. The restaurant workers were mocking me all along.

Finally, I called my psychiatrist around midnight. He said to take one more Zyprexa and to take Wednesday off work. Exhausted, I slept all day. The cloud lifted, finally, as suddenly as it had come.

Home versus Hospitalization

> Wait for the Lord;
> be strong and take heart
> and wait for the Lord.
>
> Psalm 27:14

My last hospitalization involved bizarre thinking and paranoid delusions. My diagnosis when I went into the hospital was schizoaffective disorder. This is a combination of symptoms of schizophrenia and a mood disorder.

On my way to work at the restaurant, I went to pay my bill at a department store on November 1, 2003. I saw three people getting into their car who I thought were Satanists. They were wearing dark t-shirts, had tattoos, and one was bald. Once inside, the two young people at the counter were talking about how girls and boys are always one way or another. I thought, *They know I molested boys and girls.*

On the way out to the parking lot, I came across a young man who was walking, hunched down, wearing a hooded sweatshirt. I wondered if I had molested him when he was young.

Then a car honked its horn really long like a signal. I hurried to my car and took off. Next I went to the mailbox to mail some other bills. The time of pickup seemed to be changed from what I remembered. While sitting there, all the cars on the road started honking in unison. I thought, *It must be a signal to the others about where I am.* I became frantic and could not bring myself to go to the restaurant where undetermined evil awaited me. As I drove down the street, it seemed like all the cars were converging on me. I headed toward the expressway to make it to the hospital. I couldn't go home because someone might get me. I still did not completely trust my parents. As I got on the expressway, the traffic dispersed, and I thought I was being silly. No one was trying to kill me. By this time, I realized it was my mind that was messed up and I needed the hospital more than ever.

This was the first time I had ever brought myself into emergency. My dad came down later. I was admitted shortly after. I felt funny giving up all my valuables (i.e., car keys, purse, wallet, etc.) The paranoia was to hold on for some time. My doctor had some suggestions for keeping the thoughts at bay. I hoped they would work.

1. Keep a rubber band on your wrist. Snap it when you have an intrusive thought. Say, "Stop."
2. Just say stop to yourself and move on.
3. Divert thoughts elsewhere.
4. View thoughts like watching a movie. Let them go.

When I had improved, I was moved to the less severe unit. I had a roommate who was nice enough, yet I was afraid she was going to smash my head in with the telephone while I slept. I used my lap tray to provide a barrier at night. Then I thought maybe I should kill her first, but I soon talked myself out of this idea.

After my doctor raised my Zyprexa to 10 mg at bedtime instead of 5 mg, I was more like my old self. I felt good, with no paranoia. It was time to go home.

Homeward Bound

> For the Lord your God is the one who goes with you to fight for you against your enemies to give you victory.
>
> Deuteronomy 20:4

Once home, I was greeted enthusiastically by all of my pets: three dogs, Destiny, Rudy, and Codie; and three cats, Butterscotch, Spitfire, and Baby. I felt great until night fell. I took my medicine as prescribed, yet I felt fearful that Satanists were going to come and torture me and then kill me. *This would give me a taste of my own medicine,* I thought. I had a vague sense of having committed some horrible crimes, yet I could not recall specifics.

I would sleep with my dog, Destiny, for protection. Then I'd awaken every hour to see if the torturers had come yet. This pattern had happened before. Once, many years ago, I held my mom's hand all night in her bed while waiting for the Satanists to come through the walls. Yet, every time the thought recurs, there is a new twist. This time, I was convinced I had worn a mask to commit my crimes. I also thought I had worn false teeth to prevent my bite marks from being detected. This was why I had never been caught. I was convinced that the culprits were hiding in our attic, waiting for the right time to pounce, just as I must have done to my victims.

I have lived with my parents since I left my husband in December 1991. They were sleeping, and I was sure there was someone in the attic. I knew my dad would say that no one was up there and refuse to check for me. So the thought came to my mind that the only way to get them out of the house was to set a fire. I'd have to be sure, however, to get everyone out safely. I quickly dispelled this idea, but it scared me to think that my mind could contrive such a plan.

Another fear that gripped me was that my parents were going to slip out of their bedroom window with all of my pets and leave me. Then the torturers could do their work in peace. I also thought that the people of the city of Akron would abandon me, leaving me homeless and penniless. I couldn't sleep waiting for the "inevitable." Each day that nothing terrible happened to me, the paranoia lessened. Then a new fear would arise to take its place.

One day, I awoke with a fear that when my dream state reached my waking state, I would die. I dreamed of numbers and of certain numbers bringing death. These, of course, made no sense. The panic they induced, however, was very real to me.

Thinking of the school where I used to teach prompted another delusion. I thought that I had used the school at night for my criminal escapades by impersonating the custodian to gain access to the building. Four a.m. was the target time for me. I must have taken the children from their beds, took them to school, molested them, and then killed them.

Sometimes the burden of being such a villain was too much for me to bear. That didn't stop the thoughts. If I wasn't the perpetrator, then I must be the victim. Maybe my ex-husband tied me up, put me in a cage, and took me to the school at night to perform sex acts on the staff. He may have starved me and treated me like a dog.

Then other thoughts returned. Maybe I wasn't really a teacher. My experience was all part of an F.B.I. sting operation to catch me as a pedophile. Or maybe all of the people at school were pawns in some kind of sick game. I didn't know.

Eventually, my thoughts came back to, *What's real?* and *What isn't real?* After exhausting all of the possibilities, I came back to the truth: *I have a mental illness!*

Dealing with Mental Illness

> For I am the Lord, your God who takes hold of your right hand and says to you, Do not fear; I will help you.
>
> Isaiah 41:13

Unfortunately, all of these delusions resulted in another stay in the hospital. I was working at my waitress job when I found I couldn't function. First, a woman came in to my section that looked just like my dead grandmother Starkey. I waited on her just fine, but all the while, I felt that somehow the Satanists at the restaurant had sent her to unnerve me. I stayed calm outwardly, but inwardly, fear was gripping my heart. Then another lady came in who resembled a dead friend of our family. I waited on her too. I started panicking. What did the Satanists have in store for me? Had I killed these women and they were coming back to haunt me?

I waited on additional customers, but I feared they were all mocking me. They were in cahoots with the workers, planning to kill me when the restaurant closed. Even though I had relative success as a waitress in the past, I could only wait on three tables at a time. I became frustrated easily and felt like I was being pulled in many directions.

My manager told me I was doing fine when I went to her with my concerns about my performance. I told her that I just couldn't do the job anymore. I tried for a little while longer, but it was no use. My manager had me stop waiting tables and do some cleaning. Once completed, I was free to go. I hurried to my car, expecting to be "caught" at any moment.

Once home, I expected my dog, Destiny, to come to the window when she heard my car pull up. When she failed to appear, I thought my parents had taken my pets and left for good. Then came the delusion that they had set the house to explode when I put my key in the lock. *This is what I had done in the past,* I thought, *to cover my tracks.* Now I was an arsonist as well as a pedophile in my mind.

At this point, I could not enter the house. I decided

to go back to the hospital to get help. They always helped me in the past.

Once in the emergency department, I felt safer. A psych nurse, Ed, whom I knew from years back, was assigned to my case. He talked to me about my fears and my reason for coming to the E.D. I told him of my irrational fears and how real they seemed to me at the time. While talking to him, I broke down, crying tears of frustration at having mental illness. I pondered aloud, "Why is it taking so long to get better this time?" He responded that it was common for episodes to come close together when it was time for a "tune-up." This sounded reasonable to me. My crying ceased.

This time, when I was taken upstairs, I went less severe unit, which was encouraging. This, for me, was a big improvement. I was met by a nurse who took my vitals and then took me right to my room. They told me if I had any other needs to let them know. I couldn't believe how nice they were to me. Even the unit clerk, Susan, welcomed me. I didn't know it then, but in the years to come, she would become a dear friend.

It was about 9:30 p.m., so I called my parents to let them know where I was. I had tried previously to call them from the E.D. with no luck. They were surprised at my admission so soon after the last one, but they wanted to come up and see me. They got permission from the nurse's station to come up for a short time, since visiting hours were over. I felt relieved that they hadn't booby-trapped our house and that they really wanted to see me.

The hospital routine followed as usual: early up, shower, breakfast, classes, lunch, rest, dinner, and then visiting hours. I always looked forward to seeing my parents during visiting hours. They had been so faithful in coming. Within four days, I was released. My bedtime medication was 15 mg of Zyprexa and 10 mg of Haldol. Both medications had side effects. Zyprexa made me gain forty-five pounds in nine months. Haldol made me feel like a zombie. I wanted to reduce or eliminate them as soon as possible.

I continued my work at the daycare and stayed pretty balanced. I was supposed to start at 7:00 a.m. Unfortunately, the Haldol made me very sedated in the morning, and I was often late. I missed a few days completely due to exhaustion. My boss, as always, was very understanding and let me make up my work when I could. I also cut back to three days a week: Monday, Wednesday, and Friday. I worked on an average of twenty-four hours a week. This schedule was very beneficial to me healthwise.

Focus on the Future

> And the God of all grace who called you to his eternal glory in Christ, after you have suffered a little while, will himself restore you and make you strong, firm, and steadfast.
>
> 1 Peter 5:10

Since I had been doing so well, I thought I could pursue getting a counseling degree, but I was not accepted by the University of Akron, where I had received my previous two teaching degrees. My aunt, Kay, suggested that I try chaplaincy. I called the hospital where I had been a patient so many times and spoke with the secretary of the Spiritual Care Department, Charlotte Ragan. She told me that the hospital provided the training and that she would send me an application. The application was many pages of essay questions. One of the questions was about how the applicant would be qualified to help patients. I wrote that I had overcome a chronic illness and would have empathy to those who are suffering. I was called for an interview with the director, Reverend Lin Barnett. In the interview, he asked me what chronic illness I had overcome. I told him if I did that, he probably wouldn't accept me, but I told him anyway.

Surprisingly, in September 2004, I was accepted into the Clinical Pastoral Education (CPE) program. This course provided training to become a chaplain. I had the opportunity to minister to many patients, but I felt my special calling was to minister to the mentally ill. I requested the crisis intervention unit, which was the most severe of the two psychiatric units. My director said no one had ever requested that, and he granted my request. I had great success in this area, especially with the suicidal. I went to class for five hours a week on Thursday afternoons and completed my round hours for up to twelve hours a week. Joey DeBarr, the coordinator of services, helped organize the chaplain students' round hours where the students volunteered as chaplains to visit patients on the assigned units during the week. She was always ready to listen and talk over problems both personal and professional.

CPE was sort of an on-the-job training. There were many requirements in CPE. They were labor-intensive. The required Round Hours were 190 hours per unit. There were summer intensive units, which lasted three months; fall extended units, which lasted six months; and spring very-extended units, which lasted a year. I took the very-extended units. The students were required to visit 450 patients during the unit. We had to put in a hundred and eight and a half hours on-call, which meant visiting patients throughout the hospital and answering all pages. We were called for all traumas, heart attacks (stemi alerts), strokes, code blues, deaths, as well as requested patient visits. We also delivered sweatsuits to patients who had no clothing to go home in due to the fact that their clothes were cut off in the emergency room. The psychiatric units also needed sweats for patients that didn't have a change of clothes. There were overnight shifts (from 5:00 p.m. until 8:30 a.m.) and day shifts on the weekends (from 8:30a.m. until 5:00 p.m.). The full-time staff covered the weekdays. The students helped during this time during round hours. I did my on-call hours during the weekends because my psychiatrist did not want me to mess up my sleep schedule by being up all night.

The staff on the psych units welcomed me with open arms. Better yet, they accepted me as a colleague. Many of the nurses, an occupational therapist, an art therapist, and one of the nurses' assistants who cared for me still worked there. Some of them even came to me for spiritual guidance or prayer. This has been the greatest honor for me. My friendship with the staff blossomed, and every day I work, it is a joy to go on the units. When I would open the door on the more critical side, I smelled a familiar smell of linen and disinfectant. For some reason, it comforted me. I felt at home. Unfortunately, the units were remodeled a few years ago, and with the new paint and carpeting, the smell is no longer the same.

When I became a chaplain, I found out about two important positions that I had been unaware of as a patient. They were the Director of Nursing and the Clinical Manager. They supervised the staff and patients and saw to the day-to-day workings on the psychiatric units. Kim and Pete, respectively, held these positions at that time. They also welcomed me to the floor, and were very friendly whenever I came to minister to the patients.

One of the security guards, Joel, is still at the hospital. When I first met him, he was sitting at the doorway of the more critical unit to allow passage on and off the unit. Joel has other duties throughout the hospital. One day, after my dad had received treatment in the emergency room, my parents and I met him guarding the door to the department as we were going out. My mom went up to him and put her hand on his shoulder. She said something about how well I was doing now. He said that it was great and that I was doing a good job. I said, "Yeah. They used to lock me up, and now they give me the key!" I've come full circle.

In order to do CPE, my boss at the day care adjusted my schedule to 7:00 a.m.-11:00 a.m. five days a week. This way I could do both. I started a new antipsychotic, Geodon, in July of 2004. For me, this drug had no side effects. I have been able to get up early and get to work by 7:00 a.m. I am not sleepy like before and do not take naps. I have plenty of energy and have even done some pet sitting in my spare time.

In July of 2005, I was hired as an on-call chaplain for a local children's hospital. This job required at least one unit of CPE, which I had completed by May of 2005. My work here involved mostly trauma work, which I did not really enjoy. The trade-off was that on Saturdays I got to do the spiritual wellness groups for the adolescents on the psych unit. This I loved. Most of the patients had serious problems, and I came to see how great the need with adolescents was. I did these Saturday groups until another chaplain came back from a leave and took over Saturdays. I filled in for vacations for about a year. Then, mostly, it was trauma work from 4:30 p.m. until 8:00 a.m. on call.

During this time, I continued with CPE. Because I have completed the required hours I can now be paid at the adult hospital for my on-call hours on the weekends. I usually work 8:30 a.m. to 5:00 p.m. every other Saturday and Sunday, plus some holidays. I used to volunteer to do rounds once a week for four hours.

Probably because of all of this activity, I started

having trouble with mania in September of 2006. I wasn't sleeping well, and my mind was always going. I had been working with a particularly manic patient then. One Sunday, after chapel (I do three services on Sundays, two on the psych units), a nurse asked me how it went because the patient was so manic. I told her that, to me, she seemed normal. I knew I was in trouble.

When I was telling some of the nurses about my busy schedule one day in the nurses' station, Grace G., a very wise nurse, whom I've known for years, told me I needed to have two days a week where I did absolutely nothing. This was almost impossible for me in my hypomanic state. Yet I trusted her because she had been so kind to me when I was a patient. I made a conscious decision to take better care of myself. Plus, Linda said, "Whose fault is that?" in response to my laments about how tired I was. That made me realize I was in control of how much work I took on. Those words ring true to me today when I start to overextend myself.

My doctor tried increasing my antipsychotic, but it made me too sedated. Then he tried an additional antipsychotic, Seroquel, but I had the same problem. Finally, he put me on Restoril, a sleeping medication, and I did much better. The only trouble was I slept so soundly I missed a call one night from the children's hospital. I decided in May of 2007 to resign.

I wish I could say that this was an isolated incident. It wasn't. In April of 2005, I went to Linda's house, who had just retired as an art teacher in December

2004. She, her mother, Mary, Lucy, and I still meet many Fridays at her house to do crafts, shop, or go out to eat. I have been doing this since before I went on disability in 1995. This particular Friday, I was working on a project for the daycare, which was making a display for a Latin community fair on Saturday. I was going to be there because I can speak Spanish. Linda was helping me cut out photos and backgrounds for the display board. Soon, it was near midnight, and my mom called to see if I was still there. I was so engrossed in the project that I had forgotten the time. My mom recommended that I spend the night. I really didn't want to but acquiesced.

Linda made up the bed in her extra bedroom that she had just finished painting. All of her painting materials and a step ladder were in the room. I took off my shoes and slept in my clothes. Soon after I had fallen asleep, I awoke with a start. I had to go to the bathroom. I got up and made my way to the door. I ran into the ladder and then into some other stuff. I couldn't find my way out of the room. I thought Linda had moved things on purpose to confuse me like I thought I must have done to them at their first house. I feared they were going to kill me. I managed to find my way back to the bed. I had found one shoe, and I clutched it to me. The thought came to me about what my chaplain supervisor had told me—that I was waiting for the other shoe to drop.

I lay in bed trying to calm myself but was thinking I deserved to die and go to hell. I told myself, *You know this can't be true. Try again.* This time, I felt my way to the end of the bed and went straight ahead to where the door should be. I felt the doorknob. I went downstairs to go to the bathroom. I didn't see one of her dogs on his pillow. So then I thought they had all left and were going to blow up the house. As I was going to the bathroom, I heard one of her basset hounds, Carver, coming down the steps. I felt relief—temporary relief.

I went over to his bed and petted him. Then I thought maybe I'd killed Linda and her husband or someone had and I'd be blamed. It was now 3:00 a.m. I lay down with him, petting him and crying. Soon, I got up and wrote in my organizer:

I have: Shown love to others.
Graduated from college.
Cared for my pets.
I have *not:* Killed anyone.
Tortured anyone.
Abused anyone.
Been mean to anyone.

This episode lasted about four hours. I lay with Carver until Linda got up at 7:00 a.m. I was relieved to see her. Then I talked with her about what I'd been thinking. Talking to myself in my head and talking with her all helped the feelings disappear.

On my way home the next morning, I called my doctor's emergency answering service on my cell phone. The doctor on-call called me back. He didn't seem too concerned. On Monday, I called my doctor, and he called me back at 6:00 p.m. He increased my antipsychotic (Geodon) by 60 mg a day. By July, I no longer needed the extra medicine.

Daily Grace

> But he said to me, "My grace is sufficient for you, for my power is made perfect in weakness."
>
> 2 Corinthians 12:9a

How do I face each day? I'll tell you. I try not to have great expectations because when I do, I'm usually disappointed. I just go with the flow. I pray that the Holy Spirit will lead me where God wants me to go and do what He wants me to do. This works for me from the simplest decision to the more complex. By being open to possibilities and not expecting too much, I am continually surprised and blessed by how good life is. Every day, something good happens to me, and I am grateful for it. I started a gratitude journal in 2001, and I keep a log of all of my blessings.

I believe that the only way to happiness is to get outside of yourself. Serving others gives a joy nothing else can match. Through chaplaincy, I've been especially blessed by helping others. At times, I've shared with patients certain aspects of my struggle with mental illness or my suicide attempt. I try to share what has helped me overcome, like focusing on the positive and writing affirmations for myself. Many patients have told me this helped them get through their struggle. I think the greatest thing I offer my patients is hope that the future holds healing. I encourage them to hold on and have patience because overcoming mental illness takes time. It took me twelve years.

Marianne Williamson says in *A Return to Love* that love is an energy we're born with and that fear is learned.[1] We can use love to combat our problems and conflicts. Even before reading her book, I had made my personal mission statement: "I will love as many people and animals as I can in my lifetime (and beyond.)" I try to practice love in all I do. By loving others, I find I can get outside myself and transcend any problem that seems to be pressing in at the time. Love is all that matters. When an unloving thought comes to my mind, I pray for an infusing of the Holy Spirit and for God to change my heart. I am never disappointed. Marianne Williamson suggests that we try to look at our fellow human beings as the innocent children they once were.[2] I like that.

Fear often gets in the way of loving as we should. Sometimes fear can be so great it is debilitating. Dr. Susan Jeffers book, *Feel the Fear and Do It Anyway*, helped me overcome my fears in a very real way. She recommends people take charge of their lives and find their inner power.[3] Many of the things people worry about or fear are unlikely to happen. I found this helpful in buying a home and living alone. The news is always telling us about the terrible things that are happening in the world: people are being killed, children are being molested, women are being raped, homeowners are being foreclosed upon, businesses are being swindled, and so it goes. It's no wonder every time I went out of the house, my mom said, "Be careful!" Yet, thanks to reading Dr. Jeffers's book, I have no fear. I got a mortgage during the worst possible time (and at a good rate). I am living independently. I can pay my bills. I sleep well at night because I am at peace. My friend, Linda, got me a silver necklace with a pendant for Christmas. It says, "Do not be afraid of tomorrow, for God is already there."

Because of all of the terrible things on television, I don't have cable or a satellite dish. I mainly watch my DVD's or videos that I like over again. My favorite is "The Rockford Files" with James Garner. I have all six seasons. Some of the episodes I know the dialogue by heart. I also have all of the Lassie movies plus the television series: "Lassie Celebrating 50 Years of Love."

This resulted in my love for collies and my desire to one day own one. I tried to buy one of Lassie's descendants with no reply after several letters. I also watch mysteries of Agatha Christie's Miss Marple with Joan Hickson and P.D. James' Adam Dalgliesh with Roy Marsden. Cesar Millan's "The Dog Whisperer" is another set of DVD's and videos I have. Through watching his shows and reading his books, I've been able to have a better relationship with my dogs. I can even walk all four of them at once. I wrote to him in Spanish twice with the help of *Manena,* and he sent me two autographed pictures of himself and his dogs. *Manena* also helped me translate the songs of Chayanne, a Puerto Rican singer, dancer, and actor whose love songs have left an indelible mark on me. He has quickly become my favorite secular singer. I have two of his DVD's. His videos are really works of art. I believe I have all of his CD's. I listen to him every day in my car. I also love the gospel music of Guy Penrod. His singing about God, Jesus, and our redemption always sends chills down my spine and brings a tear to my eyes no matter how often I've heard the song. Joel Osteen's Sunday broadcast is another of my favorites. His positive outlook is refreshing. The way he talks about God wanting the best for us and giving us an abundant life appeals to me. He encourages us to hold on to our dreams and not let the naysayers affect us. I have bought his first two books plus the accompanying CD's. He inspires me to reach for the stars.

People in my first unit of chaplain training used to

say that I am courageous. I don't see myself that way. I see myself as putting one foot in front of the other and trying not to get psychotic. This is my daily goal. If I can do this through loving others, then that's a bonus. It's a bonus I live for. May God's love shine through me.

Sometimes I am unable to sleep because I have so much on my mind. I occasionally have to take a sleeping pill, but the night terrors are gone. I don't fear death. The devil has no foothold in my thoughts. I think of the words of the title of MC Hammer's song: "U Can't Touch This." Satan cannot harm me because I am a child of God's. This doesn't mean the devil has stopped trying. Despite my best efforts, some "stinking thinking" creeps in. But I don't dwell on it. I counteract it by praying and by telling myself the truth, the positive things about myself. I believe in the struggle of good and evil, but I believe good wins out.

Where there is love there is God, and where there is God there is Jesus. He's there in each one of us, waiting for us to let Him into our hearts. "Here I am! I stand at the door and knock. If anyone hears my voice and opens the door, I will come in and eat with him, and he with me," (Revelation 3:20). So, in my mind, the body of Christ is bigger than is typically believed in some Christian circles. I operate from an abundance standpoint, where there is room for everyone rather than a viewpoint that excludes those deemed unworthy.

By loving unconditionally (as God does), I have

found an even greater capacity to love. The more love I give, the more love I receive. Opening myself up to love was the single most powerful force in my life. Some say you can only love others if you love yourself. I think that by loving others you validate the love potential in yourself, even when you don't feel very loveable. As I have received love from others, I've come to realize I'm all right. There is good in me. Then I reciprocate by loving others. The childhood game of "Pass It On" works here. Love increases exponentially. There is no limit. If one person loves two people a day, and those two people love two people, then those people love two people, and so on and so on (as the shampoo commercial used to say) we wouldn't have to worry about antiterrorism tactics. Is loving two people a day really so difficult? I believe love is the one thing that carries on into eternity. Heaven would not be heaven without it.

The Success Principle

> Being confident of this, that he who began a good work in you will carry it on to completion until the day of Christ Jesus.
>
> Philippians 1:6

I have been greatly influenced by the works of Matthew Kelly. In his book *The Rhythm of Life,* he advocates becoming "the best version of yourself." He contends that "success is to become who you truly are."[1] I believe this wholeheartedly.

My first episode of mental illness came as a result of years of living in incongruence. I was not being true to myself, and I hated myself for it. I have learned to live life authentically and express my feelings honestly and openly. This is my hallmark.

In my first CPE unit, I told a classmate of mine, Lorie, who is a Unitarian Universalist, that I thought I wasn't very evangelical. She said, "Can't you be evangelical by being an open, loving person?" That caused me to see myself in a much better light. I no longer felt such self-condemnation.

For years, I had felt guilty for all of the time I'd spent in bed doing nothing during my worst depressions. When I expressed this during IPR (interpersonal relations) in my first year of CPE, Eileen Schonfeld, a very wise chaplain, said it was during that time that God was healing me. That lifted a burden from my heart.

Reverend Lin Barnett helped me especially in our individual sessions. He prompted me to examine my weaknesses, and he complimented me on my areas of strength. He had a vast knowledge of books and their authors and easily recommended relevant reading. The books he suggested helped me grow as a chaplain and as a person. In class, during the verbatim section, he offered helpful critiques of my work. I took his criticisms to heart and worked hard to improve. I always felt his comments were meant to help me. They were not punitive. As a result, I improved more and more with each passing year.

My CPE friends helped immensely in my healing. They believed in me. They encouraged me. But, most of all, they loved me. From my first unit, Barbara Rose and Deb Dockery became my lifelong friends. Barbara, with her quiet wisdom, encouraged me to start my own business. She inspired me to seek my independence by moving in December 2006 to Bellingham, Washington, where she knew no one. I thought, *If she can move across the country and start a new life, surely I can move somewhere locally.* Deb, with her enthusiasm for living, inspired me to take chances in life. In her, I see a woman who has overcome great obstacles to become the successful woman she is. She grabs the bull by the horns and doesn't care if it kicks back because she has a plan to subdue it. And subdue it she does. She is fearless.

I have spoken quite a bit about my first unit of CPE. That is because it was a pivotal experience in my life. I went into CPE somewhat scared and insecure. I had a fundamentalist upbringing, which taught that we have the right way and everyone out there is a sinner. I was fearful of the world and, in my frequent paranoia, thought people were out to get me. In CPE, I found people from all faiths coming together to support one another. This was a new and wonderful experience for me. One of the most loving people I have ever met was Eileen, a Jewish chaplain. Although we were poles apart religiously, we were close at heart in our love for God. I think this is all that matters. I felt his love radiating from her in her warmth, kindness, and understanding. She is one in a million.

I remember distinctly coming out of the hospital about halfway through my first unit. I was walking across the enclosed bridge that joins the hospital with the cancer center. I had to go through this building to get to the parking deck. When I stepped onto the bridge, I was overwhelmed by a sense of peace. I was no longer afraid. I thought, *The universe it embracing me, and I am embracing it!* From that moment, I knew I was on the right path.

In 2005, I started planning to start my own business to reach the suicidal. I talked to many professionals about my idea to open a group home. They concurred that it was too high-risk. So I decided to try doing spiritual retreat seminars. I thought this was safer and was something I could do. Through Barbara Rose, a CPE friend of mine, I was put in touch with Dee Curci of The Blessed Foundation who owned a retreat house. It is a cabin in the woods on her property. I signed up to do three seminars there and set about developing my business. It is called Celebrate Life Ministries, Inc. In 2007, I applied for my 501(c)(3) with the IRS to become a nonprofit and sent in the application to the state of Ohio for nonprofit status. This process took some time. In the meantime, I had a fundraising dinner on Saturday, February 10, 2007. I invited all my family and friends and raised over $1,000. My key scripture that I had imprinted on my business checks is Romans 12:2: "…Be transformed by the renewing of your minds."

My original goal was to reach adolescents, but

I spent a great deal of money advertising with no response. Since my deadline for the first seminar was rapidly approaching, I changed gears and decided to do my June 9th seminar for adults since I knew a couple of depressed women. They both came to my first seminar, and it was a great success. I cancelled my July seminar to have more time for advertising. Yet, for my August 18th seminar, I only had one participant. She told me later she got a lot out of the seminar and it really helped her out of her depression. I was encouraged and decided to work to help people suffering from depression. I did another seminar at my church on Saturday, October 13, 2007. This time, I had three participants and the help of my pastor. My longtime friend, Barbara, from the hospital, assisted me in all three seminars. She has supported my throughout this venture. I did another seminar on February 10, 2008. This time, I had five women. It was my best so far.

In March of 2008, I graduated from my fourth unit of CPE, which was my last. IPR was a very meaningful, enriching part of CPE. IPR stood for interpersonal relations. In this group, the chaplain students, supervisor, and facilitators claimed time to discuss personal issues. The rest of the group would offer suggestions and give comfort when each one presented the problem that s/he was claiming time for. One Tuesday afternoon, October 9, 2007, I brought up that I was feeling like a failure because my business was not taking off the way I'd hoped. Kate Valentine, one of the group leaders, who was a clinical chaplain, gave me good feedback about what it means to be a success. She ran to her office and then came back and gave me a bookmark that says:

Success

To laugh often and much,
To appreciate beauty,
To find the best in others,
To leave the world a bit better,
Whether by a healthy child,
A garden patch,
Or a redeemed social condition;
To know even
One life has breathed easier
Because you have lived.
That is to have succeeded.

Author Unknown

In these terms, I know I am a success. I may not have a lot of money, but in all the ways that count, I am rich. The Gold City quartet sings, in the song, "I'm Rich," by P.L. Huffman, Jr.:

"I'm rich in faith and hope and love;
I've got more than my share;
I'll be moving to my mansion just over in Glory;
Where I'm a rightful heir."
And later the song says:

"Hallelujah! I'm a millionaire!"[2]

Throughout my CPE experience, I had many enriching experiences. The chaplains gave me support that uplifted me. All of them helped me, but a few stand out in my memory. Sister Marilyn Mihalic was a nun who was in my first and second units. We wrote midterm and final papers, which were essay questions about what we had learned in the unit as chaplains. It was a monumental task to complete. In the last question, we had to evaluate our peers and include what we called "love letters" to each one in the group. In the final for my second unit, Marilyn wrote a beautiful letter to me, likening me to a phoenix rising up from the ashes. I laminated that letter and keep it on the mirror of my dresser. In my third unit, Rachael Stinson, a fellow dog lover, likened me to a bird building its nest, thus caring for others. She gave me a small nest she found on her farm. She was also in my fourth, and final, unit and offered much support there as well. We continue to be friends today. I often relieve her on Saturday mornings that I work, and we share information about dogs and life. We both feel most at home in the company of dogs.

The love and support of my parents has been my lifeline. Without their help, I know I'd be locked up somewhere. They have supported me in all that I've done. Yet, for a long time, I'd wanted to get my own place. Financially, I had a lot of credit card debt due to spending I had done while I was in a manic state. By Christmas 2006, I had managed to pay off all my department store credit cards, and I cut them up and returned them to the stores. In 2007, I enlisted the help of my pastor to get my debt paid down. He helped me get debt-free after I'd been divorced, but I had charged over $10,000. Part of the money was for veterinary care for my pets over time.

Claudia, a nurse friend of mine from the hospital, who had once taken care of me when I was a patient, told me about a house that was for sale near her that was in the seventy thousands. This I thought I could afford if I could get a mortgage. I went to see the house with my mom's cousin, Rosemary Richards, who is a real estate agent. The house needed a lot of work. It had been built in 1913 and had a porcelain claw foot tub like my grandma Starkey's which I'd always wanted. My dad said he would help me, and some of my friends said they would help me paint. I made a low offer, which the owner countered. I came up a few thousand, but the agent said the owners got a better offer. I was disappointed.

Then my cousin found another house in the same price range on the east side of town. I had always lived on the west side. This time, my mom went with her cousin and me to see the house on Thursday, November 15, 2007. This house was built in 1930. It was everything I wanted: two bedrooms, hardwood floors, wood trim, a finished basement, and a fenced-in backyard for my dogs. Another plus was it is one block from a metro park. I decided to make my best offer, and my cousin wrote the offer right there at the dining room table. By that night, my cousin called to say the owners had accepted my offer. I had been pre-approved for a mortgage, so things were on their way. Unfortunately, after the home inspection, I found out that the wiring at this house was faulty, so I got out of the deal.

Since my disappointment was so great, I waited until the spring of 2008 to look again. By this time, my cousin Rosemary had retired as a real estate agent. I went through a couple other agents, both whom really didn't take me seriously because I didn't have a lot of money. Then, the Tuesday before Memorial Day, I had gone into the vet's office to see if they had found a home for a cat that was dropped of on Sue's, the receptionist's, doorstep because the owner had lost his job and house. They hadn't. So Jessi Llewellyn, one of the vet techs, took me back to one of the offices just to see her. The cat was a tan and black tabby about three years old. She licked my hand. Jessi said they were going to take her to the humane society because they didn't want to leave her in the office through Memorial Day weekend. Of course, I said I'd take her. Jessi said they would give her all of her shots and I could pick her up on Thursday. On my way out, I was telling Jessi about my real estate woes. She told me that her mother, Mary, was a real estate agent for Mosholder Realty and gave me her phone number. When I talked to Mary and told her what I was looking for, she told me she could help me. Within a few hours, she e-mailed me twelve properties to look at.

My previous real estate agent hadn't shown me one in over three weeks. Mary showed me many properties, yet it wasn't until mid June that I came across one that just seemed like home. It was on the west side of Akron, three miles from my parents. It was built in 1950. It was on almost a half an acre lot, which would be plenty of room for my three dogs: Destiny, Codie, and Nugget. Codie is a collie/shepherd mix who is thirteen years old. My cousin, Johnny, gave him to me on Halloween, 2003 because he was getting married and couldn't keep him. Codie is a sweet good-natured dog. He follows me everywhere like Cinnamon did. He also has soulful eyes like her. Nugget is a four year old, red brindle miniature dachshund. Linda loaned me the money to buy him from a breeder in Wooster in August of 2005 after Rudy died of hepatitis in May. Nugget likes to sleep behind my knees under the covers. He has the talent of being able to "sing." If I sing a song, he howls along. For my Aunt Mary Kay's sixty-fifth birthday, he not only sang "Happy Birthday" but he sang Elvis' "Hound Dog" since my aunt is a big Elvis fan. I even made Nugget an Elvis costume with a reversible blue and silver sequined jacket, a black wig, and sunglasses with rhinestones. Destiny, whom I've mentioned earlier, is now almost thirteen years old. She rarely leaves my side and remains my protector.

I also have two cats: Buttercup and Sugar Pie. Suzie Q ran away. Buttercup is another orange tabby. He hung around the daycare, and I fed him. One October day in 2004, it was pouring down rain, and I decided to bring him home. I kept him in the garage until I had him tested for feline leukemia and parasites. My dear cat Butterscotch had to be put to sleep right before Christmas that year for complications due to right ventricular cardiomyopathy, a heart condition that caused her to retain fluid, which, in turn, prevented her lungs from expanding. That snowy day that I took her in to the vet's, she was gasping for air. Dr. Julia Brown-Herold, the practice owner, very humanely euthanized her. Sugar Pie is a kitten I rescued for a rescue organization, Friends of Pets. She and her littermates were found in a scrap yard inside a rusty metal cabinet by a man looking for car parts. My parents and I bottle-fed her and her brother, Jet, and sister, Bootsie. Jet got adopted through Petsmart, and my parents adopted Bootsie.

I bought my house on June 27, 2008 and moved in on July first. It is white with dusty blue shutters. It has a living room, dining room, kitchen, two bedrooms, a small bathroom, and an extra finished room in the basement. I use one of the bedrooms for my office and the room in the basement for a sewing room. It has plenty of closet space for all of my clothes. I have a one-car garage and a fenced-in backyard. In September, my dad and I dug all of the holes for the fence posts with a rented auger. We mixed eighty-pound bags of cement; one for each hole. In October, my Dad put up a chain link fence on the sides of the yard and across the back. He put up scalloped vinyl fencing across the front and down the side of the drive. He finished the day before our first big snow of the year.

In May of 2009, I finally got the collie I had dreamed of having since I saw the movie "Lassie Come Home" many years ago. I bought him from a breeder, Barbara Zempel, from Barb's Collie Corner in Lynnville, Tennessee, whom I found on www.puppyfind.com. She had named him number six, but I named him Provi for Providence because God brought him to me. For his American Kennel Club registration I put Providence's Provi. He is a beautiful white and sable puppy. He has some black in his face too and a white blaze down the front just like Lassie.

I am finding life as a homeowner rewarding and challenging. I love being on my own and having things the way I like them. I love spending time with my pets. I cut back my hours at the daycare so that I could be home with them. To make extra money, I take in sewing. I still work every other weekend at the hospital. I also work Wednesday afternoons, some Friday mornings and some holidays. I don't know how much longer this will go on, however, because the hospital just had a major layoff and is cutting expenses wherever it can. But if my work at the hospital ends tomorrow, I know I have done a great service to my patients. My CPE years were a bright spot, a glowing chapter of my life. I will always remember it with fondness. It gives me great satisfaction to minister to patients who are in that dark place I once was in. I can, from experience, tell them *if I can get better, anyone can get better.*

The Upside of Living

> This is the day the Lord has made;
> Let us rejoice and be glad in it.
>
> Psalms 118:24

Joel Osteen writes, "We are victors not victims."[1] He also says that God doesn't close one door where he opens a bigger and better door. Look for the open doors. Follow the leading of the Holy Spirit on the path where God is leading. He has said he will never leave you or forsake you. Take heed to the Apostle Paul's words: "If God is for us, who can be against us?" (Romans 8:31). If we trust this promise we need not live in a spirit of fear. Dr. Susan Jeffers recommends using a "No-Lose Model" when facing decisions. She suggests writing all the positive things that can happen with any decision. Then write two signs that say, "IT REALLY DOESN'T MATTER" and "SO WHAT!

I'LL HANDLE IT!" to remind yourself whatever you choose is either inconsequential or something you can handle.[2] If the worst possible thing happens and you die, as a believer you will be with God. As the Apostle Paul says in II Corinthians 5:8, "We are confident, I say, and would prefer to be away from the body and at home with the Lord." In any case we're covered. There isn't anything that with God you can't handle.

Patients often ask me if I take medication. Yes, I do, and I still see a psychiatrist. I am not ashamed of this, yet there have been times when I tried to cut back on my medications. Each time I cut back on my antipsychotic (Geodon), I noticed I had very strange dreams, and I quickly went back to my regular dose. In the summer of 2008, I cut my mood stabilizer (Trileptal) in half. At first, I felt fine, but after a month, I became depressed. So I would recommend to people who are on psychotropic drugs to stay on them and work with their doctors to find the right balance for them. Each person is different. What works for me may not work in someone else and vice versa.

One time, when I cut back on my antipsychotic, I was on an overnight chaplain retreat. I told Becky, one of our group facilitators, who is also an occupational therapist, what I was doing. She said, "Would you cut back on your high blood pressure medications?" I realized she was right, so I went back on my regular dose that night. To people who feel ashamed to take psychotropic drugs, I would say, "Would you be ashamed to take medication for cancer or some other serious illness?" Mental illness is a disease of the brain, plain and simple. Medications are necessary to correct the chemical imbalance in the brain. I know I can't do without them. I am grateful for their help because I know I can't function properly without them. Many people don't like the side effects like weight gain and lethargy. I gained sixty pounds in the late nineties on Depakote. I know the frustration, but there are ways to combat the side effects. Working with a good psychiatrist is essential to positive recovery. By being honest with him or her about one's symptoms, a patient can help his or her doctor minimize the side effects. To lose my weight, I worked with an excellent dietician, Kim Knopp, and began to exercise in earnest. A lot is due to one's own motivation. Mine was getting over 200 pounds. With a family history of obesity, I was determined not to go that way. When I regained forty-five pounds in nine months on Zyprexa, I was discouraged. I tried on my own but could not seem to lose the weight. I asked my psychiatrist if he would write an order for me to go back to the dietician, which I did in February 2008. In a year and a half, I lost twenty pounds by eating more vegetables, reducing my portions, and walking my dogs at least a mile and a half almost every day. It can be done.

I realize that even in these modern times, there is still a stigma toward mental illness. No matter how positive I am, and no matter what success I may have, there are people who will think less of me or consider me unstable. I can't help this. I march on, happy in who I am.

Most of the time, I am almost euphoric. My psychiatrist is concerned about my becoming manic. From 2007–2009, he said I was hypomanic. Of course, I felt great during that time. Fortunately, I was not exhibiting symptoms of full-blown mania. I was not spending money, staying awake, or cleaning frantically, which were previous signs of my mania.

In March and April of 2009, I had a month of what my psychiatrist called mixed states, where I felt high and low within the same day. This was new to me. In eighteen years of having bipolar disorder, I haven't had that happen. My doctor increased my Geodon by one 80-milligram capsule. The next day, I felt much better.

I haven't mentioned much about my OCD because I haven't been bothered by it for many years. My obsession about being a pedophile is a distant memory. It helped me to work at the daycare and see those sweet children every day. I knew in my heart I could never have done those things that came to my mind. For years, every time I heard a siren, I thought, *They're coming to get me.* It wasn't until I started my chaplain training that I could hear a siren and think, *Someone needs help.*

If a person is currently suffering from mental illness, I would recommend that s/he have faith that things will get better. Believe in yourself, and find a support system that encourages you. I read somewhere that a person should imagine her/himself an island. Put on that island all of the people and things that uplift and love you. If it doesn't do that, don't put them on your island. That helped me immensely. Fill your island with the positive things and people (and pets) in your life.

People often ask me how I got better. My faith in God has been the single most important factor in my recovery. Without him, I could not have made it this far. He blessed me by bringing people into my life who supported and loved me through it all. My family, friends, and the staff at Akron General have always been there for me. Whenever I was in trouble, I knew Akron General could get me better. During the time of my most serious episodes, my mom and I would come eat breakfast in the Petite Café in Akron General on Saturdays after I had been discharged. Just being in the hospital, I felt better. I still feel that way. That is why I enjoy working there so much. My work as a chaplain is immensely fulfilling to me. Giving back to an organization that did so much for me gives me great happiness. I think the turning point for me was when I started on Geodon in the summer of 2004 and my subsequent enrollment in the CPE program at Akron General. Both of these changed my life so much for the better. The four things that helped me most were: trusting God, taking my medicine, reaching out to others, and believing in myself.

Recently, a patient, who had been in on a previous admission, came to my chapel service. He asked me to share my story with the group because he said it had helped him so much when I had told it to him privately before. Of course, I obliged. That is my mission in life and the reason I wrote this book: to tell others suffering from mental illness, "You can get better." There is light at the end of the tunnel. God can bring you through the darkness. I had a patient tell me in another chapel service that she would never get well; she would always have mental illness. I told her, "You may always have mental illness, but you don't always have to be mentally ill." I once thought the same way. I wondered, *Why am I not getting better when I'm taking my medication and I'm doing everything my doctor says?* I still don't know why. But I do know God brought me through and he is using my experience to help others. Over time, I have come to realize that we have to be willing to accept things in God's time. He knows best. Whatever trial you are going through, he can sustain you. I pray all of the time. I live in a spirit of prayer. This keeps me close to God. This past Christmas, my brother gave me a beaded pearl bracelet with inlays of silver, flat beads that say: Faith, Hope, and Love. It is a reminder of God's promises to us. As the Apostle Paul wrote in 1 Corinthians 13:13b: "But the greatest of these is love." Through love, a person can conquer any obstacle, including mental illness. All one has to do is believe and take that step of faith. God is holding your hand. Just trust him.

Epilogue

> And we know that in all things God works for the good of those who love Him, who have been called according to his purpose.
>
> Romans 8:28

In September and October of 2009, I had several psychiatric patients at Akron General tell me they didn't feel quite ready to go home upon discharge. I wished I had a sort of halfway house for them to go to get back on their feet. The Lord laid on my heart to try and find a way to do this. I also wanted to have a business where the clients could work part-time to refresh their job skills. On my way out to my friend Betty's house in Medina, I thought of a thrift store. I thought of having a big house where a thrift store could be on the bottom and the client's rooms could be on the upper level. I wanted to model the store after The Hartville Thrift Shoppe in Hartville, Ohio which is run by The Mennonite Central Committee in Akron, Pennsylvania. It is more like a boutique and very nice. Their sales go to support their missionary relief efforts. I spoke with Sarah, the manager, and she said they started in a house thirty years ago. This encouraged me.

Next I talked with Tyla, my boss at the daycare, because she has good business sense, and she is also the chairperson of my board of Celebrate Life Ministries. I wanted to incorporate this plan as part of the non-profit. Tyla recommended starting with the thrift store in order to earn money toward getting the house.

I talked with several other people about my idea. My pastor thought my plan sounded like a good idea, and he offered his support. Kathy, one of the social workers at AGMC, told me there was a need for a halfway house and that what was available in the areas were mostly group homes. Dr. Jeffries thought my idea was a good one, and he recommended I talk to a local Catholic group home for further ideas. He had confidence in me to achieve my plan. That bolstered my confidence immensely.

I am unsure how I will accomplish all of this. My stamina is not as good as most people who work full-time. But Joel Osteen said, "Don't talk to God about how big your mountains are. Talk to you mountains about how big your God is."[1] I am praying that if it is God's will, he will give me the strength. I am sending a newsletter to my supporters to enlist their help. I know I can't do it alone.

I have made it my mission to help as many people with mental illness get better as I can. I'd like to conclude this book with a letter I wrote to mental illness when I took a workshop called "Literacy for Learning" with Kim Conley of Communicate Institute the summer of 2009 to renew my teaching certificate. I shared it with Kim and some of my colleagues and they thought it was good. I also shared it with some of the patients at Akron General and they recommended putting it in this book. I got the idea from Marianne Williamson who recommended that people write a letter to their illnesses.[2]

I would recommend that those suffering from a serious illness try it because it is a very liberating. Getting my feelings toward my disease down on paper helped me to release the anger that I had been carrying all this time.

Friday
July 3, 2009

Dear Mental Illness,

I have known you for a long time. It's been over eighteen years. For twelve years you really drove me crazy. I was hospitalized fourteen times during that time, and I wondered many times if I'd ever get better. During that time, I really hated you. You took my beloved teaching career in the prime of my life for which I don't think I can ever forgive you. I don't blame you; you were just trying to survive.

I've been labeled bipolar, obsessive compulsive, and schizoaffective. In all, I was just a person trying to survive myself and not get psychotic.

The medicines I took to fight you gave me acne, caused me to gain weight, made me a zombie, and sped up the process of my developing cataracts. But now I know the side effects were worth it because now, thank God, I am well. I have been that way for nearly six years. That may not seem much to you, but it is monumental to me.

In that time, I became a chaplain ministering to patients on the psych units. For almost five years I have been helping people who are in the same dark place I once was. This is immensely rewarding to me. For this, I would gladly suffer twelve years. Giving people hope that they can get better is my mission in life.

Despite your best efforts, I am healed. I am working two jobs. I have finally gotten my own place and have been there over one year. I have written an inspirational book about my experience called: "A Work in Progress: Triumphing Over Mental Illness." That is how I feel: triumphant!

I know you are still up to your old tricks, but I'm not buying it. In the urban vernacular, "I'm not stuttin' you!" I have the tools to keep you at bay. No offense, but you've had it. I'm going to tell others how they can do it too. You can't stop me from teaching. I am educating people about mental illness. Your days are numbered. In the words of M.C. Hammer from my youth: "U Can't Touch This!"

Regards,
Sally Nitz

Endnotes

Introduction

1. National Alliance on Mental Illness, www.nami.org. 10 April 2009 <http://www.nami.org/>

2. National Institute of Mental Health, www.nimh.nih.gov. 3 May 2009 <http://www.nimh.nih.gov/index.shtml>

3. Ibid.

4. American Psychiatric Association. *Diagnostic and Statistical Manual of Mental Disorders: DSM- IV-TR,* (Washington, DC: American Psychiatric Association, 2000), 345–347.

5. National Institute of Mental Health, 3 May 2009.

Beginnings

1. Andrae Crouch, "I Didn't Think It Could Be," *The Best of Andrae Crouch and the Disciples,* (Waco, TX: Lexicon Music, Inc., 1975).

2. Matthew Kelly, *The Rhythm of Life: Living Every*

Day with Passion and Purpose, (New York: Simon & Schuster, 1999), 230.

Criminal at Large

1. *Mrs. Doubtfire,* DVD, directed by Chris Columbus (1993; Century City, CA: Twentieth Century Fox, 2006).

Daily Grace

1. Marianne Williamson, A *Return to Love: Reflections on the Principles of A Course in Miracles,* (New York: HarperPerennial, 1993), xxii.
2. Ibid, 94.
3. Susan Jeffers, *Feel the Fear and Do It Anyway,* (New York: Ballantine Books, 1987), 34–35.

The Success Principle

1. Kelly, *The Rhythm of Life,* 230.
2. P.L. Huffman, Jr., "I'm Rich," *Revival,* (Nashville: TN: New Haven Records, 2006).

The Upside of Living

1. Joel Osteen, Y*our Best Life Now: 7 Steps to Living at Your Full Potential,* (New York: Warner Faith, 2004), 35.
2. Jeffers, *Feel the Fear and Do It Anyway,* 131–132.

Epilogue

1. *Giving Birth to Your Dreams,* Television broadcast, Joel Osteen, Cleveland, OH: WEWS ABC, aired January 14, 2007.

2 Williamson, *A Return to Love,* 240–249.

Bibliography

American Psychiatric Association, *Diagnostic and Statistical Manual of Mental Disorders: DSM-IV-TR.* Washington DC: American Psychiatric Association, 2000.

Crouch, Andrae, "I Didn't Think It Could Be," *The Best of Andrae Crouch and the Disciples.* Waco, TX: Lexicon Music, Inc., 1975.

Giving Birth to Your Dreams. Television broadcast. Joel Osteen. Cleveland, OH: WEWS ABC, aired January 14, 2007.

Huffman, P.L., Jr., "I'm Rich," *Revival.* Nashville, TN: New Haven Records, 2006.

Jeffers, Susan, *Feel the Fear and Do It Anyway.* New York: Ballantine Books, 1987.

Kelly, Matthew, *The Rhythm of Life: Living Every Day with Passion and Purpose.* New York: Simon & Schuster, 1999.

Mrs. Doubtfire. DVD. Directed by Chris Columbus. 1993. Century City, CA: Twentieth Century Fox, 2006.

National Alliance on Mental Illness, www.nami.org. 10 April 2009 <http://www.nami.org/>

National Institute of Mental Health, www.nimh.nih.gov. 3 May 2009 <http://www.nimh.nih. gov/index.shtml>

Osteen, Joel, *Your Best Life Now: 7 Steps to Living at Your Full Potential.* New York: Warner Faith, 2004.

Williamson, Marianne, *A Return to Love: Reflections on the Principles of A Course in Miracles.* New York: HarperPerennial, 1993.

Praise for A Work in Progress:

Sally Nitz uses the words 'grateful,' 'blessed,' 'loved,' and 'accepted' in this narrative of her experience and recovery from mental illness. Through her faith in God and herself, the support of many who love her, medication, and the ever present compassion of her pets, Sally's story unfolds to a place of acceptance, hope, and inspiration.

—Heidi Larew, NCC, PCC-S, LICDC, ATR-BC

In this book Sally Nitz will give you a view of mental illness that is up close and personal-and very honest-not objective or theoretical. She courageously describes what her mental illness felt like from the inside, and how it complicated her life and interfered with her dreams. Yet she wants to give the reader hope in any situation-hope through faith and love. Hers is a story of triumph because of her faith, family, friends, and furry ones. As Sally says toward the end of the book: "You may always have mental illness, but you don't always have to be mentally ill."

—Rev. Verlin Barnett, L.P.C.C., ACPE Supervisor

An inspirational book! It gives hope to many struggling with this illness. Having worked with Sally for many years, it's a pleasure to see all she's accomplished. She now brings her knowledge and wisdom to our patients and helps them to believe they can and will get better. Sally's strength and courage are evident in her book and her ministry. I encourage all those involved in the mental health field to read this book to gain insight into a patient's view of this illness.

—Jeff R.N. 6400 Akron General Medical Center

This short, easily readable work in the vein of Robert Pirsig's *Zen and the Art of Motorcycle Maintenance* provides the reader strikingly clear images of the inner struggle of a psychologically disturbed young woman. It graphically depicts the conflict between her inner perceptions of her world and external realities of that world. *A Work in Progress: Triumphing Over Mental Illness* should be of particular interest to health care professionals, social workers, school counselors, and everyone who has friends, family, or associates suffering from severe psychological dysfunction.

—Ralph Darr, PhD
Professor Emeritus, The University of Akron